Spreading the Wings of Grace

KAREN SPROUSE

Inks and Bindings
888-290-5218
www.inksandbindings.com
orders@inksandbindings.com

Contents

The Confession of Karen Sprouse who came to embrace
the greater love in the midst of tribulation and trial

Foreword

I remembered every critical moment which I could not have been able to overcome, unless I would have expressed this suffering by means of my writing. Day by day when catalyzed by my grief and sorrow that would not be uprooted from my heart, I wrote.

> "Call on me in the day of trouble; I will deliver you and you shall glorify me." (Psalm 50:15)

As I recollect the time when I held fast to His word and wailed for God's redemption delivering me out of this suffering, I cannot but confess that God restored my soul, intervening in my life and staying with me. I pray that this book would be helpful to those who are agonizing over the loss of their beloveds and immersed in great sorrow, so that they could hold fast to the hope of the heavenly kingdom, by feeling God's consolation and his great and eternal love.

I would like to show my gratitude to my pastor, congregations of my church, and my friends, who have been sharing my sorrows. Moreover, I pray that I and my husband could share the fragrant love of the Christ with more and more people.

Part One

Embracing the Hope

Chapter One

Searching after a Dream

August 30th 1980, waking up earlier than usual, I just looked around the familiar scene of my room, as I lay on my bed. "I may open my eyes again in a strange place, when a day passes." A fleeting sentiment just rushed to my heart. As I thought that this was the last morning that I would experience in Korea, I could not but sense that an unidentifiable sorrow was surging up to my heart, driving me to the verge of crying.

Trying to appease mixed feelings of sadness, I started to arrange my baggage, which I had not finished packing. I packed my clothes, precious gifts given to me by my friends, and photos in two luggage bags. Then, I ate my last breakfast in Korea with my family, trying to appear nonchalant.

By 10 o'clock, a black sedan arrived at my house, which my cousin sent to take me to the airport. I just got overly excited to start such a heroic expedition, as I received a big farewell from the neighbors as well as my family. My cousin, who sent his black sedan, helped me greatly when I was in Korea. Two years later, after I came to the United States, he immigrated to the U.S. and settled in Chicago.

As I passed by fields surrounding the Kimpo Airport, everything felt so dear and special. I tried not to miss any small scenery, so that I could engrave it forever into my heart. Finally, I arrived at the Kimpo Airport. My friends and relatives already were at the airport. I looked around and there were many people who were about to part from the ties so familiar to them, weeping and holding their tears inside.

I had once been to the airport to say a farewell to my uncle who immigrated to Hawaii. But at that time, I never dreamed that I might part from my friends as well as family members. I just thought that no one knows the future. I took a picture with my friends as well as family members to remember them forever.

As the time of departure came near, when I had to part from my beloved people, tears surged and blurred my sights so much, that I could not see the faces of my friends and family. Everyone remained silent, but seemed to worry about my future. They had to accept my departure with apprehension about my going to a remote country where I may not return again, as well as with a prayerful wish for my happiness in that country. If I was going to start a new life I had to depart from the country where my heart belonged. My friends would not let go of my hands, finally we ended up embracing and the tears flowed as if they would never stop.

At that time, I began to regret my decision to choose this difficult road of separation. As it became time to depart, the announcement of boarding blast from the speaker. I got stressed by the thought that I really had to leave right away. I started walking toward the gate leaving my beloved friends and family, I took a deep breath hoping to relax as I stepped to the portal attached to the plane.

In my heart I said "Farewell to Korea!" The smell of the soil of my hometown already turned out to be a cherished memory, inciting sorrow within my heart. Sitting on the seat in the airplane, my heart grew heavy with the thought that I could not turn back. After the airplane departed from the runway, it suddenly flew on white clouds. A complicated feeling that could not be described fully immersed me into deep a melancholy.

The beautiful land, Korea, which nurtures me with pride and sense of value! The land, Korea, where I was planted sharing many things with my beloveds! My cherished hometown, which I would always miss as much as the warm bosom of my mother!

While on the airplane, I really wanted to remember my hometown in every detail. I closed my eyes and visualized it. When I was coming home from work as I stepped down from a bus at the bus stop, there was a drug store called as Chang Dong Yak Guk, and a laundry shop with a big transparent sliding door, which stood across the road. I was able to see through the door and to see the owner of the shop ironing and always maintaining the same position, whenever I came back. I would breathe out with a feeling of comfort that I finally arrived home. Whenever I saw that laundry man ironing clothes surrounded with steam, humming cheerfully, I felt a tiny piece of happiness with him. One winter day, I happened to bend over so that I could see through the frosted window. All of a sudden, my curious gaze confronted the suspicious gaze of the laundry man. He smiled at me kindly. I also smiled back awkwardly, stepping back and fleeing away, but with some sense of happiness. This warm memory on my return home fleeted through my mind.

I also could not forget the grocery store next to the laundry shop, which used to close quite late, a residential area that I passed through next to a spacious playground, and finally the unpaved road reeking with scent of soil. There I used to enjoy endless conversations with my closest friend Young Rang under a bright moonlight, and later grudgingly saying good bye to each other.

Now I was heading to an uncertain future, leaving behind my home where my cherished memories tenaciously remain. I was overwhelmed by a mixed feeling of expectation of the future as well as apprehension of the unknown world. I felt strange that I was so nonchalant about traveling to the United States for which I had always desired. It seemed that I was not ready to admit it was real.

I had been praying to God every morning for the chance to go to the United States and I felt strange that I was so nonchalant about to America about which I had always dreamed. It seemed that I was not ready to admit that the dream was real. At that time, I had some form of faith in God similar to wishful thinking that God as an absolute being might give me a reward if I prayed fervently.

Therefore, I prayed over and over that God would realize my dream of going to the U.S and thereby achieving a great success. After having made a long ado, I felt ready to apply for a visa to the U.S.A., which is the last procedure for immigration. But I failed because I did not fully prepare myself with all the documentation. Then I was given a second chance to apply for it a few days later. The night before the interview day for a visa, I was unable to sleep. After tossing and turning all night, I finally was awakened by the sound of a church bell. It seemed as if this sound awakened my dormant soul and compelled me to pray at the church. I headed to the church at the time when I usually would be sleeping.

As I passed through a darkened alley, I arrived at a broader street. At that time, I used to go to Young Gwang church, which was located a few bus stations away and far from my home. As it is little bit difficult to get there in the early morning, I decided instead to go to a small church that is located at the intersection of the street near my home. I walked to that church, determined to pray there. I looked up toward the sky, getting a breath of fresh air. The moon followed me shedding her light on me amongst the twinkling stars. Chirpings of insects interrupted the serenity of the early morning, breaking the silence of the night and culminating in a magnificent symphony.

As I entered the sanctuary of the church, I saw several people prostrating and praying silently. As it was my first experience of participating at a morning service, I sat silently on a back pew and stared at the front. Gazing at a cross hung behind an altar, I just wondered about whether God would really be present there. I tried to bow down for prostration. I just remained silent, with ceaseless tears without knowing what to pray. Finally, I prayed to God to grant a visa to the U.S.A., with desperate expectation that God already would know my circumstances. At that time, I had never read the bible and prayed only for what I desired, not for what God would want. But God had mercy on me and listened to my prayer. I was able to come to the U.S and tried to remain thankful to God for a while. But after a while, I totally forgot the grace of God.

After a long struggle, I got a visa. I once assumed that every problem would be settled, if I could get a visa. However, as soon as I got it, various apprehensions and concerns on what kind of life would await me in America overwhelmed me. I could not but perceive that another greed sprouted out after a fundamental problem had been settled. Human greed is so persistent and inexhaustible. Just as soon as I came to grip what I had desired, another bigger desire was growing. I really felt ashamed of this original sinfulness of human nature.

Finally, the airplane arrived at the Seattle Airport. I finally stepped on American ground for which I had longed. Then I transferred to an airplane going to Iowa. Looking around nervously, I purposelessly walked to the direction that people were streaming, finally arriving at a monorail station. When I got off the monorail, I found myself at the exit of the airport. I had no idea of where to go so that I would be able to transfer to an airplane bound for Iowa. I needed to ask the question "where I should transfer to the plane bound for Iowa." However, I was hesitant to ask this question, even though I had prepared myself for so many days in conversational English. Hesitating to ask a question, I saw an Asian person passing by. Chasing after him, I asked whether he was a Korean. He replied that he was a Chinese. Although I tried to explain in English showing my ticket, he did not seem to understand me. Finally, he beckoned me to follow him.

As I followed him, he introduced me to a flight attendant asking "please help this woman because she cannot speak English." I felt really embarrassed and I gave up interrupting their conversation, although I would like to express that I could speak some English. From that time on, I got on the plane and got off again, led by the flight attendant. She boarded me and other disabled seniors onto the plane in advance, before all the other passengers got on. Although it really embarrassed me, it was of great benefit to me.

I got on the plane at Seattle Airport, and I stopped over in Minneapolis and transferred to a plane bound for Sioux City. The plane bound for that city was a very small plane that can hold only 50 passengers. I really felt very sick and nauseated because I had kept eating peanuts and coke cola constantly instead of a decent meal. I really tried to endure this nausea. But as the plane kept landing and taking off over and over to take on new passengers and let them off at many different airports, I was really on the verge of dying. As the plane was quite tiny, it flew quite low. Iowa had lots of farms.

Therefore, I could hardly see any big cities and towns. I got little bit disappointed at the scenery filled with endless series of squarely-arranged farms. I was little bit apprehensive at the possibility that I might have to work at a corn farm. At any rate, this was not a scene that I had ever dreamed concerning America, I felt little bit deflated. But there is no other way than to bear it.

I finally arrived at Sioux City, totally exhausted mentally as well as physically. As I got off the plane, there was a very tiny building that looked like a terminal in the midst of a desolate field. As the airport was so small, I easily could recognize my friend and his wife as well as his children, standing in front of the entrance of the building. I was so relieved and exhilarated putting my baggage on the floor I waved my hand over my head. While I was riding in his car and chatting with him and his family, I gazed at some of the houses. It looked very strange and weird that each house had some tiny figures of chickens, rabbits, and squirrels, and mice standing on the front yard. Later, I came to know that Americans like to put small plaster-figures on their front yard. It seemed that those living in the countryside really liked to put these in their yard more than people living in the city.

As finally I arrived at my friend's home, his wife, who was a very skilled cook had already, prepared some traditional Korean food but as I was so stressed, I did not have much of appetite. I was still nauseated by traveling so long but I got better by the evening. That night, we kept chatting till midnight and then we went sleep. I had my first really deep sleep since traveling to the United States.

The apartment had two bed rooms, a living room, and kitchen, some luscious flowers showed off the skill of my friend's wife, filling the entire the living room with brightness as if these plants were artificially glazed. As they went off for work and I remained alone, I just felt confined in a strange apartment.

I was not able to do anything outside the apartment, as I was not familiar with that area and could not express myself in English. I felt strange and unfulfilled since I was used to being busy throughout the day my life in Seoul centered around many activities. As I had spent all my life in Seoul, going round and round, this leisure seemed to be so strange and unnatural. I tried to get rid of any apprehension so that I could fully enjoy this precious leisure time.

As I unpacked my bags, I remembered many things that had worried me before coming to the United States. Most of things that drove me to apprehension and anxiety seemed to be trivial. I just felt that life would be endlessly repetitive with apprehensions about such trivialities.

One day, I walked far away from the apartment and I saw quite a big field filled with various flowers. As I walked farther, I could see the twilight beginning. The twilight tinged with yellowish orange tinted all the fields and sky red, as if it was glowing. I just stood dazzled, as if I had been swirled into that mysterious twilight. The silence surrounded me. I felt as if I was standing alone in this vast world, only hearing the wind blow.

Suddenly the faces of my family and friends flashed in my mind. An indescribable nostalgia drenched my lonely heart, making me wonder "why am I standing alone, separated from my beloveds." A sorrow beyond description surged into my heart. The tears blurring my eyes were drowned out the glowing twilight.

I stayed at my friend's apartment but there was no work available in their town. My friend tried to help me find work but circumstances did not seem to be favorable. I got more and more apprehensive and felt indebted to them as two months passed. Then I found a job posting in a Korean newspaper and finally moved to Ohio. I obtained a position as a nanny for a Korean family.

This couple was so preoccupied with their business of managing several stores, from morning to evening that I was required to take care of two children. When the couple went out to work in the early morning, I had to wake up the two children; one attended a kindergarten and the other an elementary school. I would provide them with breakfast, and see them off on the school bus and give them some snacks when they returned from school. I would then help them with their homework. Since I had very little experience cooking, I regretted being unable to prepare dinner for them in the evening.

As this job did not seem to be fulfilling, I kept searching for another job by referring to the ads listed in some Korean newspapers. As I read through the ads, I came to realize that there were many various jobs in New York. I happened to get to know a friend Young-Mi. Young-Mi said that she would be willing to go to New York with me and find a job. We were supposed to go to New York after thanksgiving.

As I imagined in New York that I could go anywhere I

wanted to go by taking a bus or a subway, I just felt so liberated. I was looking forward to the day I would leave for New York and planned to live there. But suddenly Young Mi had an unexpected situation and had to remain there in Ohio. My plan to live in New York was not fulfilled.

Sometimes things just don't turn out the way we mere humans intend them too.

Chapter Two

Happiness Begins

"What God has joined together" (Mt 19:6)

One day around Thanksgiving Day, the owner of the home where I stayed lost his parents. They had to travel to another state to attend a funeral for three days with their children, leaving me alone. On the first day, I spent my time cleaning and reading some books. But on the second day, I was so anguished by my aspirations to go out, just like a bird in a cage, leaning against the window and looking at the outside.

I called Young Mi and asked her to give me a ride to the shopping mall so that I could do something different like going shopping at a department store. Young-Mi told me that it would be possible since it was her day off. Young Mi gave me a ride to the shopping mall and told me that she would come back after a couple of hours.

The atmosphere of the shopping mall was quite lively with many shoppers, before Thanksgiving Day. I just lingered around here and there for a while. And I just hurried to the place where we were supposed to meet, assuming that Young Mi might have arrived early and was waiting for me. I headed to a bench in front of the main entrance and stayed there just watching people pass by.

Then, an American man approached me, speaking to me in Japanese. I just assumed that he thought I was Japanese. I replied saying that I was a Korean, expressing my indifference to him. He apologized to me for mistaking me for Japanese, explaining that he could speak some Japanese since he stayed in Japan for a while. He explained that he intended to ask me if I needed any help, because I was sitting on the same bench since he went into the store and came back out.

As I was little bit bored waiting for Young Mi, I asked him where he came from, with my limited ability to communicate. I learned that his name was John and that he was visiting in Ohio for a holiday with his parents. He was living in Pennsylvania. He took me out on a date and while on the date I told him that I was going to move in a couple of weeks to New York for another job. John said that his place was quite near New York. He suggested that he would send me a ticket for a flight bound for Philadelphia so that I could do some sightseeing in Philadelphia and then go to New York. He said that he could give a ride to New York after assisting me with some sightseeing. John asked whether I could give him my telephone number so that he could contact me. I wrote down my phone number nonchalantly for him. John actually sent a flight ticket to me. This was the beginning of our dating. I felt that John was truthful and reliable.

I felt helpless, because I was so poor at speaking in English and could not drive. John poured out his devotion for me. With persistence and endurance, he tried to do whatever I needed to the best of his ability. Even with his devotion, I frequently felt homesick when I face some difficulties on account of the language barrier that kept me from expressing myself fully.

Sometimes I would weep for no apparent reason. I became moved by the constant devotion of John sharing my sorrow. As I was so tired and weary, his sincere kindness was a great comfort to me. I found myself relying on his devoted love and I began to love him.

John and I got married in Ohio, where his parents lived. A pastor whom my mother-in-law had known officiated at the wedding. John, a bachelor, and I, a spinster, became a married couple, when we consented to the word of God proclaiming that "they are no longer two, but one.

> "Therefore, what God has joined together,
> let man not separate. (Mt 19:6)"

Later, Soon Myung, a sister of my friend, contacted to me, saying that she was in Philadelphia with her husband who was studying at a university. Mr. Kwang Yong Han, who is ingenuous and authentic, has been a good friend to John. Soon Myung introduced me to the Young Sang church that I still attend. I had happened to go to church because Soon Myung's sister had introduced me to Christianity. And I happened to go to church in the U.S because Soon Myung also led me to the church. I believe that this is not a mere coincidence but something controlled under God's providence. I could not but feel so certain about God's love that never lets me wander and always intervenes in my life. Still, passionate tears saturate my heart whenever I recollect the providential love of God.

After 2 years of marriage, I had a child, John James, born on July 30th in 1983. We called him J.J following the acronym for his name. During the period of my pregnancy, I had many wonderful experiences feeling him budging within myself. It made me think of God's greatness. We participated in a program held by the hospital once a month with other couples and we learned how to breathe at the time of delivery, how a husband can help his pregnant wife, and what to prepare for before the birth of a child. On July 30th, I had a baby at West Chester Hospital. After I had the baby, I was so exhausted I fell asleep. When I woke up, I found John so excited at having a son at his relatively late age in comparison with others. He talked ceaselessly about how J.J looked and how cute he was. John seemed to be about to weep at the joy at being a father, saying that he talked to J.J about what he would do with him in the future. After a while, a nurse came to the room with J.J and laid him beside me so that I could nurse J.J. I raised my body and stooped over J.J and looked at him. The sharp-edged ridge of his nose resembled that of John. His large slit eyes resembled that of mine. J.J yawned and stared at me.

At that time, I trembled with an indescribably mystical feeling that I was encountering a beautiful and lovely human who embodied true humanity in his tiny body. I felt the love of maternal instinct saturating my heart. This tiny baby seemed so familiar to me like an alter-ego, calling me mom. J.J yawned gaping his tiny mouth and moving his hands and feet. We were so enraptured with his lovely presence. We could not take our eyes off of him. While feeling his tiny hands and feet, I could not but admire God's wonder. Truly, God is the one who creates all. It was the moment that I came to perceive how beautiful and precious life is. I was so grateful to God for giving us a healthy baby and making me a mother. While remaining at the hospital, I was so amazed at how American women are strong enough to walk around right after delivery, while I could not even sit, nor stand.

After three days, I went back home. John had already cleaned and polished every corner of the house. Actually, the bathtub was glittering, John cleaned so intensely for hours so that he could make the bathtub clean enough to use it for J. J's bath. However, John and I concluded that it would be better to wash J.J in the sink, because washing in the sink was more convenient for John and I to hold J.J at both sides, while washing him. We would irritate J.J so that he would wake up and we could see J. J's awakened face, but most of the time he remained asleep.

In order to protect this precious treasure that God gave to us, we did our best to care for him. As J.J was endowed with a pacific nature, he used to go all day long without crying. After I laid J.J in his crib I would go downstairs. It was my routine to listen to the sound of his breathing, and infrequent babbling through a monitor that connected between J.J.'s crib and the kitchen. Those wonderful and beautiful sounds that a tiny life made resonated in my heart with indescribable joy and happiness.

On a wintry night before J.J.'s first Christmas, a blistering wind used to shake the dried branches of the trees and make howling dreary sounds. A certain recollection of my childhood popped into my mind suddenly. At every wintry night, when I as a little girl, usually at the time I was about to fall asleep, a soliciting voice of a boy peddler could be heard selling rice cakes on the desolate street. On that night before J.J.'s first Christmas, I felt as if the gloomy voice of the boy peddler resonating through the street had sounded again.

Once in a while, my mother would buy a rice cake from the boy peddler who was totally frozen from the frigid night. I used to shed some tears because I felt so sorry for his suffering while I was enjoying this rice cake, covered snugly with a warm blanket. However, it was Christmas Eve. We gathered around the fire place, listening to some Christmas carols. This was the scene of a happy family that I always had dreamt of. This was the day when Christ was born to save all humans. I was so grateful for all the bliss that the Lord had provided for our family. At that moment, I humbly repented for my vain desire to want more and more. As I came to perceive that happiness is already embedded in a heart that can find even a small joy through gratitude, I felt some kind of joy springing from my heart that enabled me to embrace the whole world. I prayed to God, saying "Lord, please grant a peaceful and happy Christmas Eve to all those who are distressed." John was singing along to "Silent Night" that flows from the radio. I felt sanguine as I kissed J. J's cheek which was ruddy as a mellowed persimmon.

As J.J learned to walk, he also learned how to speak. Although I taught him to call me "Umma (mom in Korean)," he called me Mom in English. As I was not an insistent person, I just gave up teaching him Korean. Later, I would regret not teaching him the Korean language.

We used to buy toys to promote his intelligence. However, J.J did not seem to be interested in them, even though John tried to attract his interests by playing with them too. He liked playing with his father, but when he was sick, he always looked for his mother. I learned that a mother could be the source of happiness and the object of trust that could alleviate any anxiety and worry. Sometimes I regretted that I had not followed God, failing to entrust everything to him, unlike J.J who followed his mom. At times, I wondered whether I might have lived a more comfortable and happy life if I had been totally dependent on

God and acknowledged that my life is fully entrusted to Him.

Once, J.J caught a cold and was sick with a high fever and a ceaseless cough which made it impossible for him to sleep. As I felt sympathetic about his illness, I held him tight, carrying and embracing him. Although I gave him a fever medicine, his fever did not get better. My heart was distressed with my son's anguish that I could take on his suffering. I learned to understand the heart of my parents who raised me. I recollected the old Korean saying that "only those who come to be parents can fathom the heart of their parents." While I spent that night suffering with the pains of my son, I could not help shedding tears for my mother who had many nights like this, raising five children.

The only Korean phrase that J.J was good at speaking was "Blissful Happy New Year," a phrase that Korean people usually speak when they bow down to elders on New Year's Day (In Korean *Se-Bae*). Most of J.J friends were envious of him getting a lot of money in return for his bowing down, although they did not know what it would mean to bow down on a New Year's Day. J.J was fond of sports and thus had a lot of friends. As he was endowed with a positive mind and a kind attitude towards others because of God's grace, he lived a life of brightness and cheer.

J.J. attended a Korean church with me until the third grade, and then he started to attend an American church with his father. The church that John attended was a United Methodist church it was full of familial atmosphere. The most impressive thing that the pastor would suggest that the whole congregation have some intermittent time for collective prayers for the sake of sharing sad things as well as joyous ones and offering intercessory prayers for those who are suffering from diseases. I always thought that God would accept these prayers willingly as I stepped out of the door of the church, blessed with beautiful praises of the choir and hospitable greetings. J.J had his Confirmation at this church at the age of 13. However, I also wanted to have J.J to do his Confirmation at the Korean church where he received his infant baptism. I explained my wishes to the church and the church allowed J.J to have his Confirmation again. When J.J turned 16, he received his Confirmation again at the Young Saeng Presbyterian Church. On that day when J.J received his Confirmation, I was so thankful to God for having the names of our family listed in the Book of Life, confessing that "Lord, J.J is your child. Please guide his life according to your providential will." At that time, I thought that I fully entrusted my son to the Lord. However, my entrusting was still not sufficient. Later, I realized that I was too attached to my son. J. J's dream was to be a film director. However, he avoided going to a university in California, where he would benefit a lot in the future. I also did not want him to leave far away from home.

Therefore, we decided to have J.J study at the Penn State University that is only three hours of driving distanced from home. Before he left for the university, I requested that pastor Seong Chul Jang to come to our home and to lead a service for J.J. Pastor Jang came willingly and led a service. Our friends Jim and Eileen also attended that service. After the service, the Pastor Jang gave a lot of good advice to J.J., especially focusing on how he should have a religious life at the university, and how it is difficult to have one. He also offered an intercessory prayer for J. J's faithful life at the university. The service that we offered with thankfulness and praise was a gracious moment to all of us who attended.

I was always worried of the possibility that J.J might be neglectful of having a faithful life at the university. So, I tried to assure him that he should read the bible and offer prayers regularly. Whenever I encouraged J.J to do that, he always tried to convince me that he loved Christ as his savior and was living a prayerful life. It was my joy to hear such a confession from my son.

We went on vacation every summer with J.J. Even after he entered university, we went to Italy and Mexico traveling with him. In our life traveling together was especially blissful, a precious moment in time creating many memories. J.J. especially liked traveling on a cruise. So, he traveled to the Bahamas twice during his spring vacation. Whenever he came back home for a summer vacation, we used to spend much time together. I used to chat about his faith, friends, and various issues in the world at night, sitting on the couch and forgetting about how fast time was fleeting. Sometimes, we used to chat until the dawn.

A beautiful summer night was always too short and left insatiable attachments.

Chapter Three

Dark Clouds

"Do not be far from me, for trouble is near
and there is no one to help". (Psalm 22:11)

December 9th, 2003 Tom, a roommate of J.J called me at 9 o'clock at night. He asked whether J.J had arrived at home as he had departed from the school around four. But he said that he did not know whether J.J might come home for sure. So, I tried to call J.J.'s cell phone call but, he did not respond. Suddenly, I was seized by some sinister foreboding that penetrated my mind. It was such an indescribable feeling that I have never before experienced. This sinister premonition was so intense and haunting that my heart seemed to be frozen and my blood curdled. I came to be distressed with a premonition that something ominous and sinister had already happened. Suddenly, I remembered that J.J had come to my mind all day long on the previous day leaving my heart anxious. I had exerted every effort to dispel such a sinister premonition on the previous day. It seemed that God had trained my heart to cope with an impending hardship. I was at a loss, not knowing what to do.

After 30 minutes of silence, the phone rang. It was a

phone call from the insurance company, reporting that J.J was hospitalized because of a car accident. I stared at the frightened face of John taking the phone call. Hanging up the phone, John said to me with a trembling voice, "let's leave for the hospital." I was so shocked that I was not able to breathe. A foreboding seized my heart, I just collapsed on the couch. It was even hard to breathe because my heart pounded so fast and was aching.

Without pressing my heart, I could not even sit up. However, this was not a time for worrying about my physical condition. In spite of total ignorance of what specifically happened, I cannot deny that something ominous was approaching me. I thought that John and I would have to stay up all night at the hospital if we needed to drive there for two hours so late at night. Obsessed with the impulse that we had to leave as early as possible, we packed what were needed crazily and got into the car. On the way to the hospital located in western Maryland where J.J was reported to be hospitalized; I received a phone call from the hospital. They reported that J.J was being referred to a bigger hospital, the hospital of University of Maryland in Baltimore and they told us to come to this hospital directly. They also told us that it would take an hour to transfer J.J by helicopter to the hospital. Veering into the other direction, we headed toward the University of Maryland in Baltimore.

We were trembling with a humble vulnerability that could not have any grip on what would happen next, driving on the road shrouded with darkness as murky as our feelings. "How injured would he be?" Uneasy questions were coming out incessantly, coupled with all kinds of ominous imaginings suffocating me. I could not but feel the human vulnerability that did not have any idea of what would come to pass and the massive power of the fate in that precarious moment.

"God please heal J.J from his injuries. Without your grace and guidance, we cannot proceed further." While I was praying, I was so overwhelmed with sinister premonitions. All I could do was just call "Oh Lord, Oh Lord," with a powerless sigh. On the way to the hospital, I called Tom who lived with J.J in the same apartment, in order to inform him of the circumstances. J.J had lived with two of his friends in an apartment near the campus. As we contacted J.J three times a week, we had come to know that Tom was his closest friend.

I reported to Tom that J.J had a car accident on the way home and we were heading to the hospital without knowing the specific circumstances of his accident. And I also promised to give further updates as I learned all the circumstances. While sobbing, Tom said that he would pray for us and wished that we would drive safely drive to the hospital, saying "God bless you" It was so moving and a great comfort to us. On the way to the hospital, friends of J.J kept calling. Some of the friends who heard about the accident said that they needed to come to the hospital right away. I persuaded them not to come, not disclosing the name of the hospital. "Please wait for a while until we contact you with more information. If you guys try to drive to the hospital this late at night, we will be worried for your safety as well as the condition of J.J." By promising to give an update as soon as we came to know the circumstance, we persuaded them not to come to the hospital. We arrived at the hospital around 12:30. As we reported our names to a receptionist, she led us to the trauma center.

After passing through a winding corridor and stepping into an unfamiliar place called "the trauma center," I could see many people sitting in the dim light. There, we met a staff member and replied to their question concerning our names and insurance matters. While replying to his question, I seemed to go insane because I felt myself being caught between the sober mind requiring us to give more information and the anxious soul that worries about the injury of my son. In a waiting room downstairs, there were quite a few other people. They looked weary and tragic, leaning against chairs and staring into space aimlessly. This was a world of gloom and discomfort, different from the world of brightness and comfort that we were used too. I just could not accept the reality, imagining that I might have been thrown into some alien world fabricated in a nightmare. "Why did God help me to come to the United States, only to hurl me into this tragic misery? Why does he inflict this tribulation on me? If I were to fall asleep and wake up again, would there be a miracle erasing all these bad things?" Those questions that were arising one after another would bounce back against the wall that muffles any answer, instigating further uneasy feelings. My life that had floated over a placid sea came to get swayed and were about to be overturned by a violent storm. Assuaging the storm was far beyond my competence. I just could not but be convinced that the one who could still this storm was only God who held our life. All I could do was to pray for God's guidance over our further steps. After 10 minutes full of anxiety, I asked a staff member whether the helicopter that was bringing J.J arrived or not. However, with a distanced attitude, she urged us to stay calm until they would give further notice. There was not any other option but to wait and remain silent. It seemed that time just stopped as if just one second was as long as eternity.

Many disturbing premonitions infested my mind. After a short while, another staff member approached us. She notified us that the helicopter had just arrived and doctors would call us after they finished emergency care and examinations. She requested that we continue to wait until she would come again to lead us to J.J. I tried to ask her a question about his condition. But, again, she bluntly rebuffed my question saying that she had not received any information concerning it. There was not any other option left but to wait, ignorant of J. J's condition and how severely injured he was. In spite of the vague feeling that he might be injured severely, I still did not have any idea about his condition until I met a doctor.

I felt a strong impulse to throw open the door of trauma center so that I could see the face of my son. As I got so tense, I felt a severe pain around my chest. I tried to relieve the pain by taking a deep breath. "Why am I prohibited from visiting the ward where my son is lying?" "The rule that cannot be shattered… the custom that muffles my voice under the name of common sense…" This phrase just slipped out of my mouth. It seemed that I spent the longest night that I had ever spent in my life.

Around 3 o'clock, a nurse came to us and led us to the second floor. With my heart almost constricted, the scene waiting for me was so shocking that it made me feel as if I had been dreaming. However, it was undeniable that the one who laid on a bed and being transfused with blood was J.J. I was so frightened that I just collapsed on the floor screaming hopelessly. Nurses tried to calm me and requested that I sit on a chair, holding my tottering body. At that time, I could sense a tribulation that loomed over us as a fate with its shadowy form swooping down on me. All I could find was grave silence and fright that seemed to belie the existence of God who was my comfort. Trying to make my mind focus, I took a deep breath. I persuaded myself to remain strong to cope with all these tribulations.

John and I stared at our son J.J, holding both ends of the bed on which he lay. He was bandaged with linen around his arms, legs, and some portions of his chest. There didn't seem to be any significant injury around his face, except for some bruising around his eyebrows and lips. It seemed that he might have been severely injured, but it was hard to guess his specific injures. A young doctor who examined the X-ray results came to us and introduced himself, and requested that we move to another room and sit and talk.

The doctor reported that J.J was suffering massive hemorrhage and thus was being transfused, although he did not suffer a brain injury. He also added that the most urgent action needed was to check whether there were any internal injuries by performing exploratory surgery, as early as possible. He said that it would take some time to prepare for the operation by normalizing his body temperature, since he was cold from the helicopter flight. The doctor recommended that we sit around J.J and to keep speaking to him so that our presence could make him relax and help him recover his consciousness, even though he had been sedated. The doctor tried to comfort us by encouraging us.

Heaters were installed to raise J. J's body temperature and were shedding light upon his injured body. Although I was half out of my mind, I sensed that J.J seemed to try to open his eyes. Seeing his attempt to open his eyes I whispered to him. I awoke, with some small hope that he might recover from his injuries, by means of recent medical technology which arose out of my desperate feeling. His somewhat infrequent bodily response to our address revived some hope for his recovery. I whispered to J.J, saying that "J.J, God will raise you up again because God so loved you. That is the reason why you have to pray to God for salvation.

You should not forget that God has always loved you." I was just murmuring, while weeping and sobbing. Tears were dropping out of my eyes and flowing over my cheek ceaselessly. "Oh God please hold fast our hands so that we could overcome such difficulty." Withholding some words that could not slip out of my mouth, I just stood silently gripping the frame of the bed. Suddenly, I could hear the sobbing voice of John who had been sitting on the opposite side of the bed. "J.J., I love you. And I need you.

Please do your best. Struggle for your recovery with all your strength! You have to get well. Never give up. I cannot live without you." That desperate voice resonated in my ear like an echo that may have resounded out of a certain alien world, far off from this miserable reality. I wanted to assure J.J that I was staying with him by embracing his injured body. But I could not do this because of a respirator machine and tubes installed around J.J. I was really cautious of not touching any of those numerous tubes connected to the body of J.J that were transmitting medicines and blood. I kissed his ears numerous times. I could sense his temperature as well as his heart. "Oh God, please let me have all this pain instead of my son. Why did I live a daily life with such a haughty mind, assuming that misery has nothing to do with me?

I am such a foolish person. Please forgive the many sins that I may have committed inadvertently as well as advertently. And please forgive my excessive love of my Son J.J... I dare not bargain with you for his life, requesting that you take my life instead of J. J's. Everything is under your sovereignty. Please have pity on our family." As I offered the prayer of confession of my sins, I sensed some peace was emerging from such a desperate feeling.

John and I were caressing J. J's wounded hands, standing on both sides of the bed. Surprisingly, J.J tried to open his eyes and looked at us with his eyes half open, noticing that we were there with him. As his moves looked so painful, I just told him to stay calm and comfortable with his eyes closed, as we knew that he was listening to us whether his eyes were closed or not. I also tried to comfort him saying that John and I would never leave him and many doctors at this huge hospital were trying their best to recover his health.

At that moment, tears were flowing out of his eyes. Did J.J respond to the passionate love of his mother? As J. J's body shuddered, his temperature went up by 1.1 degrees. Many nurses standing around J.J were exclaiming, and indicated that he could be moved to the operating room. I exclaimed also, shouting "God! Thank you So much!"

Chapter Four

Why Me?

Like Birds hovering overhead (Isaiah, 31:5)

December 10th, 2003 Around 7 o'clock, J.J was delivered to surgery. It was reported that the surgery would be done by groups of doctors assigned to different parts of injuries. We were in the waiting room for hours while J.J was getting surgery. Intermittently, doctors came to us and got our signatures for the consent for different surgeries, and reporting the progress of his condition. Sometimes, they reported that his life was put in danger.

We were just oscillating between hope and despair, according to what doctors reported to us, in accordance with J. J's hovering between life and death in the surgery room. It was so painful to sit on a chair powerlessly and have no idea of how J.J. my alter ego was suffering in surgery. Although I sat up all night and all day and did not sleep at all, my mind was alert because of my anxiety. I was just leaning back on the bench. All I could do was to breathe like a person in a vegetative state.

After 5 o'clock, J.J was delivered back to the ward. A nurse led us to the ward where he was sent. Following the nurse, I stepped into the intensive care unit. In the room located down the end of a corridor, I could see J.J lying there. As I stepped into the ward, I could see my beloved son sleeping peacefully, covered with a blanket as white as snow but still equipped with a respirator. The nurse reported that he would be transfused because of the loss of blood and the progress of his condition would be under constant watch. Silently, we watched over the external injuries, standing on the both sides of the bed. A doctor stepped into the room and explained the progress of the surgery.

He reported that the result was quite promising because there were no internal injuries in the abdomen. But he also added that the result of the surgery done on the injuries in J. J's left leg seemed to be unclear. However, he stated that the surgery itself was perfectly done. That gave us a great comfort and my heart was little bit eased. Because of the doctor's remarks, it seemed that I had just come out of a winding tunnel of darkness into a bright world. Now I could have some room to look around at the circumstances. Of the various machines surrounding J.J, we could recognize a machine that gauged heart beat and a respirator that provided oxygen to his lungs.

We stood beside the bed adamantly observing how his heart beat. Although the nurses urged us to rest, we kept insisting on sticking to this spot. Finally, they stopped trying to persuade us to take a rest. We were standing there in the same posture just as J.J was sleeping the same all day long. Although I had stayed up all night without taking even a little nap, I could not feel any fatigue. Rather, my mind got increasingly active. We were supposed to go out of the ward for 30 minutes for nurses to exchange shifts. Around 8 o'clock, a new nurse took up her position. Although the visiting hours were restricted until 9, she took the trouble to allow us to remain until 10. When 10 o'clock arrived, she said that we were not allowed to remain in the room any longer, and persuaded us to take a rest.

We went back to the hotel. Although the hotel was located quite near to the hospital, we were so exhausted that we took a taxi. I felt as if thousands of years had passed in just one day. As I stepped into the hotel room, I felt as if my mind filled with despair, deserted my body. It felt benumbed and paralyzed. I just fell on the bed and hoped that God would perform a miracle if I would wake up after a long sleep. I happened to smile faintly, envisioning that God would be healing my son with his curing hands. Like birds hovering overhead, the Lord almighty will shield… (Isaiah 31:5)

December 11th, 2003 John and I woke up at dawn, simultaneously. John called a nurse and asked about the condition of J.J. The nurse replied that his condition had not changed since we left the hospital. In the early morning, we went back to the hospital by walking a few blocks. I could see many doctors and nurses who had worked all night conversing with each other while eating some breakfast. We also ate some food against our will. Then, we stopped at the chapel waiting for visiting hours. It was soundproof, free from any external noise and quite serene. Pews polished with many years of prayerful presences of people welcomed us.

We held hands tightly and prayed to God. It occurred to me that God was testing us without listening to us, in spite of our desperate prayers. Suddenly a Bible passage: "You of little faith why do you doubt. (Mt 14:31)" came to my mind. I felt frustrated at my distrust of God. Suddenly, I heard John sobbing. Who would embrace his collapsing heart? It seemed that no one else except God could heal his wounded heart. His suffering that had been repressed because he comforted my sorrow just erupted. The world full of hope and joy turned out to be a gloomy and painful one. The future turned out to be a mass of despair and clogged up our life. I could not elicit any clear answer out of all the messy questions. The most prominent one out of these was the question of "why is God allowing this tribulation to happen to me?"

At that time, a doctor who just finished his rounds was passing by us. We tried to request that he give more specific explanations concerning the physical condition of J.J. However, all he said was that we have to wait and see, not giving an answer that we would like to hear from him.

J.J seemed to sleep peacefully. When he had been a baby, we used to watch him sleeping beside his bed for a long time as we were now doing at this hospital. Suddenly the memory of that day 20 years before was come to mind, transcending time and space. When I had been watching baby J.J sleeping in a cradle, his saliva often slipped out of his lips and sometimes made tiny bubbles. Now, out of his lips, a feeble thread of his saliva was streaming. Sometimes, nurses removed the saliva through a suction tube. I volunteered to do that task. I could not help doing something of benefit for him. Watching him all day long, we would come back to the hotel, only to stay awake with insomnia.

December 12th, 2003 J.J started another day without having any progress, and suffering painfully. As I walked into the hospital, the corridor was crowded with people and the cafeteria was filled with a lively atmosphere. Except for J.J, everything seemed to remain normal. It seemed to be only my family that was struggling to survive in a world that had been totally changed.

I happened to meet the doctor in charge of J.J. While passing by, he decided to come back and give an encouraging remark, "That a more aged man would not have survived if he had been injured as severely as J.J". He also added that the circumstance was very promising because J.J was young and healthy. We were so glad to hear that, smiling at his remark. I could not give up any hope, obsessed with thinking that I had to save him. "I should be strong. I should be strong." I used to speak to myself several times a day as if I was doing a self-hypnosis.

I would wonder how capacious my heart is, that God endowed me with. As it is said that God permitted a suffering that is bearable, it occurred to me that God would grant me a capacious heart that could handle this tragedy. However, sorrow burst out too often for me to repress it. My heart really ached as sorrows pressed it. Suddenly, tears surged up like a spring without any control. We were nothing but an injured animal groaning in order to protect its suckling. I once had a chance of hearing a desperate groaning of a beast somewhere in the deepest part of a mountain. Crying bitterly and groaning similar to that of an injured beast sounded out of my heart.

Free me from the trap that is set for me, for you are my refuge. (Psalm 31:4) But I trust in you, O LORD; I say, "You are my God." (Psalm 31:14) For in the day of trouble he will keep me safe in his dwelling; he will hide me in the shelter of his tabernacle and set me high upon a rock. (Psalm 27:5)

I wrote down these phrases on the bed frame where J.J was laid and read them whenever it was possible for me to do. John and I tried to meditate on this word, which was also our desperate prayer. Today, when I spent the whole day reading the book of Isaiah and Psalms, it occurred to me that various phrases of the Scripture that sounded only intellectual came to be the living Word of God that was touching my heart. Every verse was piercing my heart as a living Word, arousing my soul, and then opened my eyes that could gaze only at God even in my severe misery. Various words of the Scripture came to flow out of my heart as my true confession. I read them over and over, repenting my previous life. I could sense the Holy Spirit healing my broken heart and comforting me at every moment.

Some nurses felt pity on me, seeing me reading Scriptural phrases and praying for J.J while holding his hands. They suggested that they would read the phrases to J.J while we were away. Another nurse promised that she would take care of J.J as she would her own child, saying that she was also a Christian. Phillip, one of those nurses, cordially reported, that he already had taken J.J as his adopted son within his heart. It was such a beautiful scene that many souls could share love united in Jesus. A nurse named Jenny in charge of J.J told me that she could not sleep well at home, on the day when J.J arrived in such a bad state. She witnessed that she exerted her best for J.J since he reminded her of her 20-year-old son. Those nurses taking care of J.J with sincerity seemed to be angels. John and I received a great comfort from them. We offered a prayer of thankfulness to God.

December 13th, 2003 Pastor and junior pastors visited the ward. I was so thankful for their coming in spite of the two-hour drive. Pastor Yong Gul Lee seemed to be seized with a deep sorrow while he was stepping into the ward. In order to control his emotions, he opened and closed his bible over and over, finally only to burst out shedding tears. His humane and merciful heart really gave a great comfort to me. The missionary, Myung Duk Kim, was also so tender to her congregation like a mother. I could not but burst out crying, embracing him. The tears of love shed in Jesus thawed my stricken heart and gave a great comfort.

On that day, I had been a bit frustrated as J.J did not get better. However, I felt empowered by the messages and the prayers of pastors. Different than usual, I found myself reliant on pastors like a wandering sheep as I came to face a crisis. I need as many spiritual supporters as I could get. And I would like to beg a prayer from anyone else. As I saw J.J not making any significant progress, it occurred to me that the period of J. J's sufferings might last more than I expected. Moreover, it also occurred to me that there is not anything that is more precious than life, as I came to perceive the world from the perspective of the forked road between life and death. Everything that I had valued suddenly came to appear as trivial and insignificant. I cannot but dismiss my previous life obsessed with various trivialities.

John informed our relatives of J. J's condition and requested that they pray for his recovery. His relatives reported that they were praying together with the members of the church that they attend. John's church was praying for J. J's recovery as well as the Korean congregation of the church that I attended. Especially, the pastor of the church that our friend the Thompson's went to was said to inquire about the condition of J.J, even though the pastor was himself hospitalized in the emergency room. I was so thankful for prayers of that pastor as I heard the story. I also prayed for his recovery. Even my friends in Korea comforted me with prayers.

I could sense that we were living everyday by the power of prayers. I received an e-mail that 10 congregations altogether were praying for J. J's recovery. I was so thankful to God for sending those warriors of prayers. It really occurred to me that the church, the community that God provided to me, was so beautiful. I came to perceive what it means that the love of Jesus Christ binds all of us into one in God and every member of the church comes to be into one body in Christ. God does not leave those who are distressed and stricken alone, but sent many spiritual supporters to pray together, and shed the power to us through which we can sustain our daily life.

December 15th, 2003. We asked to the doctor in charge of J. J's case about what would be the most critical to J. J's condition. The doctor said that there are still some bacteria floating in J. J's blood, adding that they were unable to identify its source and continued to examine it, although they kept treating it with antibiotics. He reported that the bacteria infiltrated J. J's leg. My heart was so disheartened. It was so unbelievable that microscopic bacteria infiltrated into the body of J.J and could paralyze the whole body of a robust young man. I could not but understand that the human body is so fragile.

I stooped over and scrutinized J. J's leg again; he had been a prominent sprinter. I could not estimate the condition of the right leg, as it was in a plaster cast, while that of the left leg seemed to be fine. However, what the doctors said was totally different from my guess. They said that sinews of the left leg were greatly damaged and thus more serious than the right leg. I held J. J's two feet and prayed to God. "Oh God! Please restore both legs of J.J as they had been and let him live for the sake of the glory of God for the rest of his life, standing firmly on his two legs.

I believe that you will raise J.J up. I tried to pray with certainty. But I found myself being shaken by my little faith. I really felt so guilty of my little faith, as I assumed that it might delay J. J's recovery. I spent this day going back and forth between the ward and the chapel. In front of the chapel, there stood a great picture reminding me of some beautiful pasture with a light behind it. I felt as if I stood in the midst of that pasture. This place could provide significant moments of rest through our prayer and rest. It functioned as a harbor and shelter that empowered us. However, J.J was not awakened, shattering our expectation that he would recover consciousness after the surgery.

We had stayed for several days at a hotel near the hospital. Whenever we entered the hospital, we came with some hope that J.J might have regained his consciousness while we were away from the hospital, but only to be disappointed. As J.J seemed to be in a stable condition with his temperature normal, John and I decided to go home in the evening to pack some clean cloths and organize the mail. Although I arrived home in the late evening, I could not concentrate as I kept worrying about J.J. I opened up mail sent to us. John's company sent him a card. John had not been able to go to work for many days, thus leaving many things undone. John's colleagues sent a card of consolation, encouraging John not to care about the work but to focus on taking care of John. I read through many cards that expressed the wishes of many people praying for the recovery of J.J., I thought that J.J should recover soon and respond to the expectations of those who had concerns for him.

John called nurses every two hours, having some intermittent naps. He was even thankful for J. J's condition's being the same as we departed from the hospital. One concern the nurse had was that J. J's temperature did not go down, even though they medicated him for a high temperature. She added that this was something usual that would happen after a serious surgery.

That night, I could not fall asleep, my heart was troubled and disturbed thinking about J. J's cold toes that I had touched.

I held his toes in my hands tightly and massaged them so that I could warm them. I wish I could have warmed his toes somehow; I would have even thawed his toes by putting them in my mouth. As I tossed and turned to make myself fall asleep, I suddenly felt dizziness and fatigue, unable to budge any part of my body. As I closed my eyes, I felt my soul and body being swirled into a dark whirl, hurled into somewhere that seemed as dark as it can be. That night, God provided us with a deep sleep that brought us a necessary rest.

Chapter Five

Mom! I Love You

No temptation has seized you except what
is common to man. And God is faithful; he
will not let you be tempted beyond what
you can bear. But when you are tempted, he
will also provide a way out so that you can
stand up under it. (1 Corinthians 10:13)

December 16th, 2003. Suddenly, the phone rang with a clamor breaking the perfect stillness of the night. An earsplitting sound awakened me, bringing unspeakable fears. "Something may have happened while we were sleeping." I handed the phone to John with a trembling hand, guessing that something urgent might have happened. I could overhear what the doctor was saying to John. He said that they had to amputate one of J. J's legs in order to save his life and they needed an oral consent by phone as he did not have enough time to wait for our written consent. We were at a loss in such a pressing situation.

We just told them to save J. J's life at any cost and promised them that we would come back as early as we could. Then, we just headed toward the hospital with our best speed. The chill air of an early morning scarred my heart with its merciless frigidity, instilling a cruel sorrow, instead of the usual freshness. He might lose his leg…it seemed that what we had feared might happen came to be realized. All we could do was to wish for something miraculous that may happen while we were heading to the hospital. Knowing that there was not anything that we could change, but we still could not let God lead us to whatever would come to pass.

We were just groping for a way, wandering in the midst of thick haze. The haze gets thicker and thicker blinding any visibility, only to suffocate me. As we arrived at the hospital, a staff member said that J.J was already in the operating room. We could hardly breathe; we collapsed on the couch in a waiting room feeling defeated. "Where is the future of my family heading?" I tried to cling to God so that he could give me enough power to sustain these unbearable moments filled with the misery of floating around in the dark ocean without hope.

After a while, a doctor wearing a burgundy gown stepped into the waiting room and bringing a chair sat next to us close. That young doctor came, loosening his interlaced fingers and covering his face with his big hands. And then, rubbing his hands again and covering his face again, he showed some signals that he had a difficult thing to announce. We just looked at him, soliciting his immediate response. Then, the doctor turned toward us and gazed at us with his congested eyes. My heart was throbbing, waiting for a verdict that he may give to us.

The doctor opened his mouth, saying that he was sorry to report sad news. He said that the operating team had to amputate one of his legs, as infection would spread infecting other parts of his body risking his life. With an unbearable shock, I felt like screaming "Oh My God." However, that cry just came to be muffled within my bruised heart, not letting me speak anything. I would like to ask more questions. But I collapsed as if I had lost my life. I could not move any part of my body just as if I were oppressed. I felt dizzy as if my energy were sapped out of my body. I thought to myself that my soul would leave my body at the end of my life just like this. As much as my soul crumbled, so did my body.

I just got stunned for a while. I regained my consciousness after a while and found John as if he was frozen hard covering his tear-stained face with his hands. We were so defeated that we did not have any power to sustain each other. I wish I could hold his hand. But I could not do it. John also seemed to be really shocked as much as I was. He did not seem to recognize that I was sitting next to him. The time of grave silence lasted so long. J.J. must have been the best friend of John, as he begot his son at the age of 39. J.J was the one whom John must have loved the most. After an hour, a nurse arrived to bring us to J.J. Then, I got sober. I felt a strong maternal instinct surging from me, inspiring me to cope with all the difficulties.

I prayed silently. "Dear Lord, I know that you're my master the only one who can raise me up. Please make whole my shattered soul. Please heal my soul with your hand that can heal all broken hearts. Please sustain my soul and body that collapsed again. Please give us the power to cope with all these difficulties." After finishing this prayer, I took hold of John's hand firmly like a warrior waiting for a battle. We should be strong for our child. These two hands interlaced with each other are the strongest hands in the world with which parents are holding fast for the sake of their children. We stepped into the ward. I could see the peaceful face of J.J forgetting any turmoil. "How hard it might have been for him!" As I looked into the face of J.J, my tears were flowing because I was so happy to see his face again.

John and I immediately thanked God for saving J. J's life. My son was breathing in front of us. We could not ask any more than this. As we gave up many things and left all to God at this crisis of life, thankfulness overflowed in that J.J was still breathing. We really got comfort from a doctor's remark that he could even run in the near future, if he was equipped with an artificial leg. It occurred to me that my thankfulness overflowing from my heart in the midst of this tribulation was only possible because the Holy Spirit remained in my heart. As I stepped out of the hospital, each life that I encountered was really moving and aroused some sense of unity. I offered a prayer of thankfulness to God who sustained me in such an unbearable moment.

> "No temptation has seized you except what is common to man. And God is faithful; he will not let you be tempted beyond what you can bear. But when you are tempted, he will also provide a way out so that you can stand up under it. **(1 Corinthians 10:13)**"

December 17th, 2003 As we came back to the hospital, a counselor was waiting for us. An older man who looked gentle said that he had worked as a counselor at this hospital all his life. As his long career might suggest, he seemed able to look though our anxieties. Moreover, he also helped us to evoke various questions that we had to ask concerning how to cope with these difficulties. We had had no idea of how J.J might get through all these difficulties and overcome his sufferings.

The counselor comforted us that this hospital provided many rehabilitation programs inspiring motivation, providing counseling, and helping a patient to recover.

One of the most impressive programs was to match patients with various mentors who had already succeeded in rehabilitation and thus could share their successful experiences. I was even more moved by his remark that those mentors were all volunteers. I was so ashamed of my life full of self-centeredness. I have never paid any attention to the issue of disability. Understanding that my son was disabled, I came to have much interest and concern in those who are disabled. When I encountered anyone who used a wheel chair, I could not pass by but always pondered about how hard he or she might have struggled in his or her own life. I could not but applaud their courageous struggles.

God opened a new world to me. I had had no concern in the many disabled people who had to struggle on account of their accidents or their idiosyncrasies. I had never thought of the possibility that the issue of disability would fall on my life. I could not but repent my past sins of being indifferent and negligent to my neighbors who were suffering themselves. God helped me to repent those past sins, making me realize that I had been the disabled one whose heart was impaired with self-love and pride. I determined to feel more love and concern for those who are disabled while I lived.

We started to encourage each other and pray together as one body more than ever, thinking that there would not be any one else than two of us, John and I. Therefore, we did our best in sustaining our health, mindful of my determination that we should not get weary until J.J could also stand firm again.

December, 18th, 2003 We came to the ward, as early as the visiting hour began at 9 o'clock. After listening to a short report from the nurse taking care of J.J, I was staying with J.J until 10, when I had to get out of the ward as the nurses had a duty rotation. I went outside and sat on a bench next to a fountain installed in the central corridor of the first floor. As I looked into the water of the fountain, I came to identify myself with the water that kept surging up and pouring down constantly. It seemed that my heart that surged up with hope and collapsed down with despair was quite similar to the rising water of the fountain.

As J. J's swollen face got increasingly better, I could see the face of my son that I had been familiar with. We just left the hospital after giving a good night kiss on his bandaged leg. After coming back to my hotel room, I started to write down all the Words from the Scripture that had given me and John great comfort. I really wanted to share these Words with J.J if he would regain his consciousness.

"So do not fear, for I am with you; do not be dismayed, for I am your God. I will strengthen you and help you; I will uphold you with my righteous right hand. (Isaiah 41:10)"

This Word brought me ineffable comfort and thankfulness again. The wounded love of God toward me also permeated my sorrowful heart. As the pain stuck deep down within me broke apart tears surged out endlessly. I felt my soul purified, as tears filled with sorrow and comfort washed all those unclean things inside me, pouring joy on my heart. I could sense certainly that God really had mercy on me and would protect me by keeping his eyes on me. The certainty of God's love came to fill my depleted heart. "God… Please protect my son tonight!" I entrusted J.J to God and fell into a deep sleep early in the morning.

"But I trust in you, O LORD; I say,
you are my God. (Psalm 31:14)."

December 19th 2003 Ten days had passed since J.J was hospitalized. It seemed that John and I had gone through a murky tunnel of despair. But one thing was clear; we had been relying on only God in the midst of unfathomable darkness. And we also came to perceive that we could not make any step further without God's guidance, especially if we did not entrust everything to God. We were relieved that J.J. no longer had a high fever. I washed his body with a wet towel. We thought that we could go home for a moment in order to get fresh clothes and repack our personal items. We left for home with a reluctant heart because we were leaving J.J alone.

It got dark outside and I could see some stars in the sky. Stars were shinning in the onyx sky. It was not that cold. I could see some Christmas trees decorated with some candles shining in various forms. The moon hung in the sky shining forth its orange light as a decoration that God had set.

December 20th, 2003 John left for the hospital in the early morning. I decided that I would go to the hospital in the evening with Hyun Soo my brother. John called me around 2 o'clock. He urgently said that J. J's condition had worsened since we left the night before and urged me to come to the hospital immediately.

I collapsed once again. I did not have any power to stand upright. I collapsed and thought about the Korean proverb, "Mountain over mountain." I foolishly thought that I already went up over the mountain, presuming that all I had to do was merely continue only to find that there was another mountain to cross. I had no idea of why things were going bad even though we gave up one of his legs. While I was trembling with fear of an impending danger, the phone rang. It was Pastor Lee asking about J. J's condition. Pastor Lee advised me to entrust everything to God as life and death was totally up to God. Repenting my little faith, I opened the bible placed on the table and read any passage randomly. I happened upon Psalm 55.

> "O God, do not ignore my plea; hear me and answer me. My thoughts trouble me and I am distraught at the voice of the enemy, at the stares of the wicked; for they bring down suffering upon me and revile me in their anger. My heart is in anguish within me; the terrors of death assail me. Fear and trembling have beset me; horror has overwhelmed me. I said, oh, that I had the wings of a dove! I would fly away and be at rest— (Psalm 55:1-6)"

While reading the verse; "Oh, that I had the wings of a dove! I would fly away and be at rest," I was crying and waling. That afternoon, I left for the hospital with my brother Hyun Soo. On the way to the hospital, Hyun Soo suggested that J.J might be weary so we should become another leg for him. With a sobbing voice, Hyun Soo said that he would be another foot for J.J. Hyun Soo owned a drycleaner. Hyun Soo said that he could run the business with his agile feet while J.J could make his living by managing the shop with his smart brain. Hyun Soo tried to keep comforting me. I thought to myself that sympathy is the most precious gift that God endowed to mankind. As we arrived at the hospital, John was waiting for us. He smiled at us brightly. He reported that J. J's condition had gotten better and his fever subsided for the last couple of hours. John's face looked tired, reflecting his agony for the day.

December 22nd, 2003 Relishing fresh wintry air, we came to the hospital a little refreshed. Dropping in on the chapel for a prayer, we later stepped into the ward and met J.J. There I felt a sense of thankfulness that I could still hold his hands and look into his face and we be together. I was deeply immersed in this profound happiness wrought by God's grace.

Around five o'clock Jim, Eileen and their daughter Caitlin came to visit. I had a good friendship with Eileen as she shared a similar personality and character, i.e., being emotional and sensitive. Eileen and I were similar in that we could empathize with suffering of others easily. We would weep and sob on account of a story of suffering of other people. I could sense that cordiality could be felt beyond the boundary of race and language. They comforted me and promised to take J.J as their child and to do their best for J.J. They gave me all the support that a family could give.

I came back to the hotel after staying with J.J until 10 PM. I brought some Christmas presents that I had bought for relatives. I changed my mind and gave these gifts to the staff at the hospital. I wrapped each gift, arranging them on the floor. Envisioning each face of various staff members, I tried to express my thankfulness for their help with the Christmas cards and gifts.

With these gifts a tiny expression of my thankfulness, I felt a strong impulse to bring the love of Jesus to them. There were a few non-believing nurses and doctors. Hesitating about what to write, I wrote down the phrase "May God's love, be with you." I really prayed that they would experience the love of God in their lives and God's grace would remain with them.

December 23rd 2003, I expressed my gratitude to all the

staff that I met for their considerate services. Some of them even hugged and encouraged me, showing their sympathy. I felt myself having an eye for looking into people's hearts, as I could sense what others had in their minds, even though they did not fully express themselves verbally. I thought to myself that anyone with a sympathetic heart was blessed and beautiful.

J.J did not seem to be awake, still sleeping. However, I could see that he moved his arms occasionally and tried to open his eyes. As his eyebrow was swollen, I applied some ointment to him. I also washed his face with a towel. He seemed to regain consciousness enough to hear what I was saying. I told J.J to open his eyes if he could hear me. As soon as I spoke, J.J exerted himself; he moved his eyelids and finally opened his eyes for a few seconds. Suddenly a tear dropped out of his eyes. His one move really seemed to be extremely painful. I thought that each tiny move might be the most painful struggle for him. I was so grateful for this tiny gesture that he made, pouring out all his energies. His tears seemed to speak one thing silently. "Mom, I love you!"

Part Two

In the Midst of the Valley of Tribulation

Chapter Six

Christmas

"Surely goodness and love will follow me all
the days of my life, and I will dwell in the
house of the LORD forever. (Psalm 23:6)

December 24th 2003, we met with the doctor before I saw J.J. We pleaded with the doctor to give us more information because we really wanted to know what J. J's condition was like. I asked the doctor whether they found the source from which the bacteria were propagating. He replied that it was really difficult to find the source and they were doing their best to find it. He said that they would replace tubes with new ones and do a CAT scan again around his abdomen and would inform us of the result as early as it could be done. We observed every single word and gesture of the doctors and nurses and kept asking many questions. In spite of my inquires, they always responded to me with kindness. However, they also replied that there were lots of things that they could not tell me. How could a human who was not God foretell what would happen? I found I was so desperate to gain the slightest clue from them. Actually, I was so grateful for them for doing their best in saving J.J.

Every Christmas Eve, J.J used to make us laugh when he shook the boxes of presents laid next to the Christmas tree or when he was caught sneaking some presents to be given to John and me into the house. He always made me happy as he laughed out loud, full of embarrassment. As many memories of the good old days occurred to my mind, I could not but have a faint smile. Those happy memories inevitably made the current situation much gloomier.

Sitting on both sides of the bed and looking into the face of J.J, John and I talked to him telling him many future plans when he recovered. We promised to buy him a new TV set as well as a brand-new computer. We also promised to equip him with an artificial leg that would be the most comfortable one in the world. We also swore that we would never make him clean his room for the time being at least. Laughing and sobbing while talking about various promises, it came to be the time for nurses to rotate their positions.

We went down to the chapel of the hospital to have a worship service at 7:30. As we entered the chapel, a chaplain welcomed us. There were two women, one couple and their two children and their mother. They said that the husband of the old woman had had a car accident 21 years ago and had remained in a vegetative state for a long time. However, the husband of the old woman was said to regain his consciousness miraculously on a Christmas Eve. The pastor also explained that their family kept celebrating that miraculous day on every Christmas Eve.

It was said that the Christmas worship at this chapel had been led by the pastors of the local community and some retired pastors in rotation. We had a short time of sharing our experiences. A pastor who came late listened to our sharing of experiences suggested that he give a benediction to all of us. After asking about our wishes, he gave each of us benediction with zeal and sincerity. Praying together with zeal and passion for each other, we were thankful that God opened our hearts to each other and made us pray for each other as one body. I sensed that God would surely accept this beautiful worship and our cordial concord in this tiny chapel. At this moment, I found myself practicing the commandment of Lord, i.e., "Love one another just as I loved all of you."

After the worship ended, the pastor asked about in which ward J.J was hospitalized. I let him know the ward number and its location. Some minutes after we went up to the ward, the pastor visited J.J.'s ward and prayed for J. J's recovery while holding our hands. God gave a comfort to us by sending this pastor on this lonely night. We had a night full of grace as we felt the comforting hands of God on this silent and holy night.

December 25th 2003, we came back to the ward, at the visiting time in the morning. Although it was Christmas today, J.J. did not wake up like a sleepyhead. I kissed his brow and greeted him with my best cheery "Merry Christmas." Then, I whispered "God bless you" a thousand times. In the afternoon, my brother and sisters brought their children to the hospital in order for us to enjoy this Christmas season together. My nephews and nieces seemed to be astonished at hearing that their cousin, who used to play with them, was deeply injured and suffering in the ward, thus unable to play with them.

We decided not to bring the children into the ward to prevent them from being shocked. I stayed with the children in the waiting room while the rest of adults went up to the ward. All of them seemed to be joyous as they gathered together. As I was watching children playing cheerfully and joyfully, I could sense that a joyous Christmas atmosphere was near to me. As the hospital waiting room seemed to be so crowded, we decided to move to the hotel. There the children could play in a more spacious room they were so thrilled and cheered. Still, I could see that family is really important to me. I could not but be thankful to my brother and sisters who came from remote places just to be sharing my suffering. We stood making a circle and prayed together that God would protect J.J. with all our zeal.

Eating some food that my siblings brought and chatting with each other, I really had a wonderful time. My brother insisted that he stay further but I persuading him to go back home. I walked back from the hotel to the hospital. It got dark and started to drizzle, foreboding a gloomy future. Christmas! And the one who came to this earth on this day to take the sins of all people and to save those perishables from their sins. Suddenly, I was overwhelmed with God's love that is beyond human imagination and understanding. The day, on which the blessings came down to all people! There were lots of homeless people. I could see many homeless people sitting on the corner of the street. I crossed the road intentionally and gave some money to each of them, praying that their lives could be more blissful. I could not simply overlook them as each of them bears God's precious life. It is because I came to perceive how precious the life of each individual was. I decided that I should love more people around me whom I may meet in my life. I raised my arm up to the sky, wishing that God would hold my hand perpetually, feeling that God would look down at me silently from some corner of the dark sky.

December 26th, 2003 Pastor Lee, and other church friends came to the hospital and we had a worship service led by the pastor in the chapel.

"He said, 'If you listen carefully to the voice of
the LORD your God and do what is right in his
eyes, if you pay attention to his commands and
keep all his decrees, I will not bring on you any of
the diseases I brought on the Egyptians, for I am
the LORD, who heals you' (Exodus 15:26)."

The pastor preached about this verse. We accepted this Word into our heart affirming "Amen." I determined to have trust in and entrust my life to the providence of God that would always lead my life to a good purpose. We prayed with our voices, united as one. I was so thankful to my pastors and friends who came to the hospital in spite of their busy life as well as the long distance between the hospital and their neighborhoods. Once again, I could ascertain that the life of the church community was deeply entrenched in my life in the form of the love and comfort that they shed on me.

Because it was the Christmas season, more and more visitors came to the hospital, surrounding us with a busy and cheerful atmosphere. Even though I felt some loneliness in the corner of my heart, I felt that someday God would lead me out of this deep tribulation and suffering to the green pastures. Also, I felt some peace of mind springing out because God is always with me.

December 29th, 2003 I persistently conceived of a possibility that J.J would welcome us in the ward, regaining his consciousness, whenever I woke up in the morning. Every time I came to the hospital with a slight hope that he might regain his consciousness, I ended up disappointed when I saw him remaining unconscious in the bed. It did not take a long time for me to accept the cruel reality and to abandon any hope for a miracle. It occurred to my mind that J.J.'s struggle might last longer than I expected, as I saw him bedridden.

We got accustomed to staying at the hospital as well as at the hotel. It became our daily routine to wake up in the morning, to walk three blocks to the hospital, then to pray silently at the chapel, to eat breakfast, and to wait for the visiting hours reading the bible and asking about the progress of other patients from their family members.

The hospital provided a counseling program for the sake of patients, that was served by various counselors and religious leaders who helped patients and their family members to solve the problems, in so far as patients and their family members requested spiritual support from them in advance. Not only religious leaders but also counselors were available at any time, even accompanied by interpreters. A counselor whom we had met once visited us in the morning. She asked how we were doing and told us that they would transfer J.J. when he was ready to another hospital that was near to our neighborhood. They had already contacted a person who had lost his leg in a car accident and had completed the rehabilitation programs and made a successful progress, so that he could give good advice and support to J.J. The counselor added that he would help J.J recover from the shock of losing his leg and to get accustomed to all the changes that would occur. I could not but be amazed at how well this program was organized. I felt thankful that J.J was treated in such a good hospital. I even felt inspired by the idea that it would be more comfortable to transfer J.J. to the hospital nearest to my house and it would be done very soon.

In the afternoon, John and I came back home to take care of the mail and packing some fresh clothes. John left home for the hospital before dark, after having taken a short nap. I decided to stay home that night and would leave for the hospital with Hyun Soo the next day. John called me from the hospital in the evening, reporting that J.J.'s condition suddenly got worse. As I could not drive to the hospital alone, I tried to ask Soon Myung to drive me to the hospital. Unfortunately, she was very sick and thus unable to drive. I was at a loss to know what to do.

Coincidently, I received a phone call from the wife of Pastor Jang, Eun Jin Park. She contacted me saying that with pastor Jang they could give me a ride to the hospital. He drove me to the hospital, and I felt deeply indebted to his kindness; I also sensed that the presence of the pastor would give great support to me.

As I arrived at the hospital in the late evening, John was waiting for me. It turned out that J.J. also had a yeast infection in his blood. I was at a loss at what to say. There was not anything that I could do. Even the doctors did not have any answers. Were all these hopeful remarks that doctors had given us just irresponsible promises? There was not any answer given, just distrust against doctors as well as anger toward them. I could not help but admit that a human is only vulnerable to God's providence and what I can do is only to seek his mercy with zeal. Pastor Jang, who remained polite and gentle all the time, explained about things that God would do beyond human comprehension and understanding. Every word he uttered was warm and tender, shedding his sincere love to his sheep. As I listened to the theological remarks of the pastor, my perturbed heart stilled and regained its peace. As it was too late to go back home, I encouraged Pastor Jang to stay at the hotel for a night and to leave for his home early in the morning.

As Pastor Jang consented to my suggestion, I reserved two more rooms for Soon Myung as well as the pastor. As Pastor

Jang and I were members of the same church cell group when he was a lay person, I was bit more familiar and comfortable with him. Moreover, his presence was really supportive and comforting to me. I decided to stay overnight at the hospital and then to rotate with John in the next morning, as I really wanted to stay with J.J that night. Dissuading John from remaining at the hospital overnight, I tried to persuade the three of them to go to the hotel.

Originally, it was prohibited for anyone except for staff members to stay in the ward after 10. However, I solicited a nurse so persistently; she agreed that I could stay overnight. I was so stupid that I did not notice his heart beating irregularly. I could never imagine that J.J would leave us on the next day. All I did was clean his body with wet towels and read some bible passages to him. I also sang some hymns to him. I could see tears running out of his eyes. I just could not figure out why God made me experience such a heart rendering love.

All I could do was to pray for God's mercy clinging to him totally. God inspired the power for me to sing and pray ceaselessly overnight. I pleaded for God's mercy on J.J.'s soul with all my tears. I pressed my cheek against J.J.'s cheek. Tears kept overflowing down both our cheeks. As I thought back to that night, I felt it was the final worship directed toward the heaven. It seemed that God prepared and allowed one more night for a mom and her son to worship together, before he would take J.J to the heavens. I kept praying and praising overnight as people would do in a revival meeting. J.J also shed lots of tears as if he had been aware of it.

These tears might be the tears of repentance to God as well as those of love for John and me. I was so happy as well as sad, joyous as well as painful as I would worship God overnight with my beloved son. "Dear God, how painful had you been when your son was inflicted with incomparable sufferings. People were so evil, stubborn, and ignorant that they crucified you on the cross. I humbly confess that I am really a miserable sinner. But Lord! My heart is so aching and frightened that I cannot sustain myself any longer. Please have mercy on me."

It became morning. Nurses seemed to get busy with making up reports notifying what had happened overnight. The nurse who had taken care of J.J last night was sitting on a chair and making up his report. John entered the ward around 7, to take his turn. Although I stayed up overnight, my mind was never exhausted but robust and clear. Moreover, my spirit was saturated with the grace that I received yesterday.

As I was walking out of the ward, I met Pastor Jang and Soon Myung. I smiled at Soon Myung and told them to go back home with the pastor after having breakfast. As I came back to the hotel, I suddenly felt fatigue surging up. I just fell on the bed and slept, even without changing my clothes. After a couple of hours, the phone rang. As I answered the phone, John urged me to come to the hospital immediately, whispering with a trembling voice. "Maybe…Maybe…" I suddenly felt a great dizziness. I just hung up and sat absent mindedly. "How can it happen that my son might die? Should I go there where my son is dying?" I wished I had been able to disappear if possible. I would like to avoid the reality of my son's dying. This hesitation disappeared so quickly. I was seized with an urgent impulse to see J.J immediately. I got out of the hotel crazily and got in a taxi. As I looked out from the taxi, the world was the same as it always was, crowded with people coming and going. Suddenly I felt myself isolated from the rest of the world, feeling inexpressible loneliness and solitude.

"Surely goodness and love will follow me all the days of my life, and I will dwell in the house of the LORD forever." (Psalm 23:6)

Chapter Seven

The Last Kiss

"Meaningless! Meaningless!" says the
Teacher. "Utterly meaningless! Everything
is meaningless." (Ecclesiastes 1:2)"

December 30th, 2003 As I arrived at the ward, everyone including the doctors, nurses, John, Pastor Jang and Soon Myung surrounded J.J., watching the electrocardiogram signifying irregular beating of his heart. I approached him, trying to stand firmly in spite of trembling legs and looking at him. We remained silent as if we were accomplices to his death, guilty of his death. "Oh God, I cannot part from my son.

Please let him live even though he may become vegetative! I will be thankful to you even though I will see him in such a condition." Even in this last moment, I tried to cling to my hopeless prayer and begged God for his miracle, saying that I could not give him up in this way. This might be the final cry of maternity that tried not to lose just one string of the relationship between a mother and a child. At any cost, I did not want to lose this string of a relationship with J.J until the end of my life. I really could not let go of my hold of his hand even though I may lose my life. J.J.'s heart beat got more irregular.

Even though I could see that there would be no turning from his death, I murmured absent mindedly. "Oh God! Please take my heart out of my body and put it into J.J.'s chest instead! Take me to the heaven instead of him!" This desperate plea was merely muffled in my throat, only to give way to a hopeless sigh. Suddenly, John held tightly to my hand. And he enunciated with desperate determination. "J.J.! You do not have to struggle anymore. You may go to heaven now. Commend your soul to God. Let us meet in heaven! I will see you there. The happiest moments of my life were when I was with you. I really love you more than anything!" John's tears were dropping on the hand of J.J. How could parents bear to see their child die before their own life ends? We were just merely humans who could not prolong even a tiny bit of his life. Life was such a fragile thing… As soon as John made a farewell call to his son, J.J. ceased unbelievably to breathe. And soon as the heart beating irregularly ceased to pulsate, a flat line came to persist on the screen of the electrocardiogram. Gazing at the screen absent mindedly, I just fell down on J.J.'s chest, covering his body. I stopped thinking I went blank.

I kissed my final fair well to J.J. "J.J. This may not be the last meeting. We will see you again. Please have a good time in the heaven, where there will be no suffering. Life is not that long. I will see you very soon at the place where you are. I will be there. You will live in my spirit until I die." I whispered my sorrow into his ear and leaned over his chest. I could sense his warmth. "Why could I not feel his heart beating?"

A doctor notified us that the body of J.J would be delivered to a mortuary after he signed the death certificate. Sitting on the chair and staring at J.J, we could not admit that he was dead. Some strange ideas were lingering in my mind, as I could not admit the reality. I kept wishing that I had been able to take J.J to somewhere else. Ignoring any kind of customs and constraints, I wished to keep J. J's body near to me. I also wished that God had taken me with J.J to the heaven. I could not but realize that everything was vain and futile. I still collapsed on the floor totally void of any emotion, as if I had been anesthetized in my spirit and feeling that what had happened was not real.

As Pastor Jang was in charge of funeral services related to members of the congregation, he prepared for everything on my behalf. Pastor Sun Man Kim administered the final service at the hospital. After waiting for a doctor's signature for confirmation of J. J's death for an hour, John and I went back home, leaving my son at the hospital. Pastor Jang said that a mortuary contracted with our church would come to the hospital and finish all the procedures for death notice. (My son no longer existed in this world.) On the way home, I felt so much pain trying to repress my impulse to return to the hospital and to see his face, while thinking that I could not touch or feel him anymore. It was really hard to hold back my urge to request that John turn back to the hospital. Many cars were going by everyone seemed so busy. How fragile a human is! What are they striving for!

"Meaningless! Meaningless!" says the
Teacher. "Utterly meaningless! Everything
is meaningless." (Ecclesiastes 1:2)"

The word that spun around my mind was this verse. I felt like I did not belong anywhere. Everything that I saw had no meaning. I would not see him anymore which gave me a feeling of despair, loss and disillusion making me feel completely hollow. After coming home, I just lingered around the bleak garden, as I could not stand these feelings. While standing in the garden a cold wind blew and I thought the empty shell of my body would just fade away. Ceaselessly the cold wind blew though my body Whooo whooo! I heard that wind blowing though me all day long.

January 1st, 2004, we sat hopelessly on the couch on New Year's Day when we used to have fun gathering together, chatting and eating some special food. Shocked at the death of J.J, my siblings also stayed at their home not knowing what to do. Around 10, Mrs. Park and Elder Hong visited us bringing a variety of delicious foods. Although, we had been devastated, we started to regain our balance by their great support and comfort. I can never forget their consideration and love.

January 2nd, 2004, we had to prepare for something we could not even imagine, J.J.'s funeral. My church had bought a block of cemetery plots for its members. They did not have a grave plot for a family but only provided a spot to each individual according to sequence of their death. However, as there were three unoccupied spots on the margin of the church cemetery block, we decided to buy these for our family. Coincidentally, there was a grave for my mother in the same row. J.J. would be buried with his grandmother. I could not help but to wear a bitter smile, thinking that God was so considerate.

We also purchased the burial plots for us. There was nothing left for us to do to make J.J stay with us in the world. A staff member of the mortuary asked us how we would arrange the formation of graves. John and I replied unanimously "Please put him in the middle between us." We would like to have J.J between us that is all we can do in this world. He told us to bring some clothes for J.J. to wear and some personal items to bury with him. I chose a suit and his well-thumbed bible. I also picked a cross-shaped pendant and his cell phone that he really had liked as his favorite. Then I brought them to the mortuary. I just wished that J.J might call me back saying "Hi Mom," if I put his cell phone in his coffin. I'm thinking to myself at that moment "am I losing my mind, am I going crazy…"

We had to make funeral arrangements, we had to choose his coffin and the Scriptural passage inscribed on a tombstone. We had to do many things we really did not want to do. I thought that it would be my last chance to do something for J.J. I could not help but try to give to J.J the best that I could. I really wished that I had more time to prepare myself for this separation. But I already fully knew that this would not happen. Just today I did not want to think about custom I just wanted to stay with JJ all day but I knew that I would never be ready to let him go.

We had the viewing service at the small chapel in Washington Memorial Park. Pastor Yong Gol Lee and Pastor George Tigh led the service. J. J's close friends came and displayed various pictures that they had taken with him. I could see J.J.'s friends embracing and comforting each other, they all had been devastated at the loss of their closest friend. J.J.'s friends standing around him made their farewells with their utmost bitterness and sorrow. Most of J.J.'s close high school friends came to the funeral, as they had been back to their home from college for winter vacation. J.J.'s college friends also came, driving really far from their own places. Many people came including John's brothers, colleagues, church fellows, and J.J.'s previous teachers, to express their condolences to us. Suddenly, Richard, J.J.'s former roommate, came and embraced us sullenly, sobbing and crying. All I could do was pat him on his back.

January 3rd, 2004 a wintry morning and a frigid wind was blowing! I wished to expose my heart to this frigid blast so that it could become numb, frozen with this icy wind. Before leaving for the burial place, we had the funeral service at the chapel. After this service, we stepped toward the small place where he would be laid. His burial place was within a ten-minute walk. Following the funeral limousine carrying J.J., many cars were heading toward the burial place in a procession.

I got out of the car and watched as his six closest friends unloaded and carried cautiously the coffin decorated with many red roses. J.J. was taking the lead in advance of all of us on the road where no one could escape. I also followed the step of my son, who was traveling on his last road in this world. Following J.J.'s friends carrying the coffin, I was little bit worried about whether they might feel the frigid cold. I could see them carrying the coffin with one hand while wiping their tears away with the other hand. Their sorrow really lacerated my heart again. Yes. I lost not only my precious son but they lost their dearest friend. In our life, those who had shared love with J.J. became unable to share their love with him any longer. All the people who shared love with J.J were following him mournfully and sorrowfully.

The hill surrounded by trees similar to a folding screen was full of silence like our hearts sedated with our deepest sorrow. Only the sound of the footsteps and the sound of a wind blowing around us could be heard intermittently. The frosty wintry weather permeated even under our clothes, making the mournful hearts feel more frozen with sorrow and sadness. J.J.'s friends put the coffin cautiously on the spot prepared for burial. There was a tent, under which we would hold the final service before burial. J.J.'s coffin was placed in the middle between the seats prepared for his family. The tent had been already installed to protect the coffin from snow and wind.

It came to be the time for holding the burial service facing the final separation in this world. Pastor Lee gave a short sermon; we sang a hymn surrounding the coffin and placed a rose on it. The red roses held by people having loved J.J. were piled up and scattered on the coffin, dispersed like my bloody tears. "The relation between mom and son, a desperate tie that connects me to my son whose hand I cannot hold again!" I could not avoid the moment that I had to walk down from the hill and turning around I would leave J.J. alone. I could not die at the moment; I really did not want to lose my hold of the tie that connected me with my son until the end of my life. There is nothing I could do; I just closed my eyes with painful silence and kissed his coffin for a final farewell. Tears running out of my eyes were splashed back to my face by the fierce wintry blast. Mrs. Eun Hye Lee, who was the wife of the pastor, gave her arm to me and helped me turn from the coffin of J.J. I felt a great comfort from her embrace like a child in the bosom of his mother. J.J.'s friends wept with me, while introducing themselves to me. They embraced me and mourned with me.

I really could not converse with them and tell them what they meant to me by their mourning. I really wanted to spend more time with J.J.'s friends. The time was so limited. How can I bury him in a grave? How can I turn away from this place, leaving J.J. alone? I really hated the custom of the world that forced J.J. to be buried in an isolated place and compelled me to come away from J.J with others, leaving him alone.

Leaving him alone in the cold grave, that night I could not sleep as I wandered around in my illusion like a sleepwalker.

My imagination that J.J. might suffer from being chilled and frozen in that lonely dreary place in this frigid night; really seemed to drive me to get out of the bed and to come to the cemetery and be with him. I was really groaning. "How can I sleep in such a warm room while my son is outside in the cold?" I was really beside myself. I groaned over and over as the sorrow inside me formed a lump nearly suffocating me. I tried to muffle this sound of groaning; this catalyst of sorrow totally permeated my whole body and paralyzed my rationality. I wailed and writhing over and over until I got exhausted. While trying to soothe my sufferings, John also burst out crying.

As I looked out the window, I could see a tree standing in the back yard. I could see the tree struggling with a relentless blast wind of a winter night, with its branches ceaselessly rattling in spite of its strong trunk. A feeling of unquenchable sorrow erupted as I identified myself with one of those weak rattling branches. I spent that interminable night fighting against the frigid blast just as the branch did outside. That night was so long that I thought the morning would never come.

January 4th, 2004 John and I could not sleep all through the night. As soon as the sun rose, we ran to the Washington Memorial Park, where J.J was buried. The place where J.J was laid was covered with roses and flowers. They were frozen with frost like pieces of ice sculptures. I felt my heart lacerated as I thought that my beloved son had been buried under such cold soil. Grass had turned white with frost but still sustained its life in this frigid soil. In the frosty sky, a flock of birds flew away. John and I stood still in this desolate dark field, facing a breeze blowing out of the dawning sky. I felt like I was thrown into a harsh place that I had not known on this earth.

The desperate heart turned out to be unbearable sorrow.

"I am standing on the earth! Where is he? A strange situation in which the world has not changed at all, but only my son disappeared!" My heart was so painful as if it had been pierced with something. I looked up to the sky like an insentient hollow person. How far is the heaven from here? John and I looked at each other with tear-stained eyes. We could sympathize with each other. We just embraced. John called the name of J.J. wailing. "My Son J.J." That desperate cry echoed in the dawning sky. "Oh God! This is real punishment. Why have you only left the two of us here? It is such an unbearable tribulation!" A frigid wind seemed to paralyze my hands and feet. I wished that time had stopped. I wanted to be frozen like a block of ice.

Chapter Eight

The New Habit

"In all your ways acknowledge him, and he will make your paths straight" (Proverbs 3:6)"

January 10th, 2004 as my mind weakened, I could sense that my body also collapsed, silently. I could not fall asleep no matter how I tried. My body ached and suffered from fever. I would wake on account of this pain and fever. Moreover, my gums got swollen and my teeth got so loose that I could only eat food with unbearable difficulty.

I visited my dentist a couple of months after my last visit. He said that this was caused by stress. The dentist said that the widow of the deceased Pastor Young Suk Lee visited him for the same symptom that I was suffering, i.e., loose teeth. Pastor Young Suk Lee, a pastor of my church Yong Saeng Church died, leaving all the prayers and love of the congregation behind. At that time all the congregations were grieving for him at the tribulation of the bereft family, the young widow and her three children. I felt so sorry for Mrs. Lee's agony, a bereft widow, who suffered the same symptom as I did, I assumed that she also got through such a severe emotional struggle caused by the loss of her husband as I did. I could not forget the kindness and sympathy of Mrs. Lee who deigned to come to the funeral service of J.J. in spite of her own suffering and pains.

January 13th, 2004. "So, I hated life, because the work that is done under the sun was grievous to me. All of it is meaningless, a chasing after the wind." (Ecclesiastes 2:17)

My body got weak and wearier; I could sense that my spirit got more devastated. Every night I had a fever and my body was stiff all over and I sweated a lot. One day, I found my bed soaked with my sweats. I tried to do my best to recover by myself, as I did not want John to worry about my struggles. He had his own to worry about.

All the beautiful scenery in the world lost its life force. It looked unreal just like a scene in a picture book. The only thing that inspired life to me was being with my husband John. I didn't care if I lived or not but we had to live so that we could help each other. We were united in the passion and sense of duty of protecting each other from those sufferings that enervated us. We encouraged each other "to live righteously and thus to go to heaven so that we could see J.J. there again." It would be really frustrating for J.J and us to separate from each other in such a meaningless way. We were still seized by the question; what kind of meaning could our further lives have, if we could not see J.J. again?

January 17th, 2004. Our focus of life was not in this world but in heaven. I spent all day thinking about heaven. I only struggled to pick up some passages relevant to the theme of heaven, while reading the Scripture. Nonetheless, I would doubt about the existence of the heaven once in a while. Does the heaven exist? Did J.J. really go to heaven? What kind of appearance would we have, when we met each other in heaven?

A habit of looking to the sky grew within me. A beautiful

blue sky made my heart feel painful and aching. The dusky sky made my soul depressed and sorrowful. A dark cloud made me feel despair. The days of agonizing over the existence of heaven and the loss of J.J. continued. I felt myself stuck with this problem. I could not read the Scripture, nor offer prayers. I felt powerless as if there were not anything that I could do for myself. My close friend Soon Ja sent a sincere letter of comfort. She wrote that she would pray for me adding that she could fully sympathize with my feeling of total powerlessness. I thought about the many people who were praying for John and I, worrying about our life. The beautiful love shared in the life of Christ really enlivened and inspired us. We realized that all of those people who's caring and love gradually but ceaselessly helped us recover from our despair. The portion in our life reserved for J.J was large. A part of our future was lost. I had never even thought about a life without my son. The purpose of my life remained hopeless and aimless as if I was lost. It was merely a life of survival, day by day.

January 18th, 2004. I could not sense anything because I lost my five senses. All I could do was just sit and stare aimlessly throughout the day and then lay down sleeplessly every night. My body gradually deteriorated. I suffered head aches every other day. My muscles kinked internally and afflicted me whenever I tried to move. It was really painful for me even to raise one arm. Once in my bed, it was really difficult to turn over. Some friends invited me to dinner to comfort me. I was very reluctant and refused their invitations, although I was so thankful for them. I was neither excited nor interested in the outer world. All I did was just to wait for the time when the great sorrow might end.

Two of my friends insisted on having breakfast with me,

although I persistently tried to reject the offer. I was led by these two close friends who wanted me to get out in the fresh morning air and have breakfast with them. Laughing and chatting with friends at the coffee table made me feel better. Stepping out of house, I saw an azalea which endured the cold weather. The persistence of the azalea persevering in its mission to survive the winter gave a beautiful inspiration to me. Like that azalea, I wished to persevere in front of God's eyes.

January 29th, 2004 the insurance company contacted me, reporting that J.J.'s car was in their custody at a car yard. They said that they would scrap the car only after a family member would take the private possessions of J.J. and sign a form. We knew that we had to do these things. But we kept procrastinating, as we would like to avoid another reminder of J.J.'s death. At first, John said that he would go there by himself. However, after couple of days, he said that he could not go there, saying that he was not prepared yet to face J.J.'s car.

Thankfully, John's colleague, Tom, who knew our situation well, suggested that he could take care of everything related to the car, saying that he was accustomed to doing those kinds of things, as he had worked as an emergency medical technician. Tom insisted on going alone and taking care of those various things by himself for us, in spite of John's suggestion to accompany him. Tom deigning to drive the long distance alone took care of all these things for us. We were concerned about each other so we tried not to show our individual pain in order not to hurt each other so we chose to absorb our pain in silence.

January 30th, 2004 there was another painful thing left

that we had to take care of. We had to take J.J.'s personal items out of his apartment. It sounded really tragic even to think of going to the apartment and packing his personal items. We tried to procrastinate as long as we could but we could not avoid it. My brother Hyun Soo and John decided to go there. Thankfully, J.J.'s roommates suggested that they could pack J.J.'s possessions for us. We could not let them fully take on such a burden. However, their help in some of the packing really saved much time.

February 1st, 2004 in the early morning, Hyun Soo drove with John sitting next to him to the apartment near the Penn State University where J.J. used to live, in order to pick up his personal items. It took three and half hours to get there, only one way, thus a total of 7 hours for the round trip. Although they left really early in the dawn, they came back around 3 PM far later than it was supposed to be. John said that they spent some more time with J.J.'s roommates.

I fretted about their coming home late just as I had done when I had waited for J.J, walking around here and there in the house. I looked outside, whenever I heard a car coming. I was really anxious about confronting J.J.'s possessions that he used to use. I murmured all day long, saying "God help me! God help me!" As I think about how painful John might feel when he was packing up the personal items at the apartment, it was so painful and heart wrenching to let John suffer these things. I prostrated and prayed to God, "Lord please give comfort to John." Around 3, I heard a car stopped in front of the house. It seemed that John and Hyun Soo came back. As soon as I opened the door, I was so shocked that my heart felt frozen. I could see those familiar clothes of my son. Hyun Soo just bores these clothes on his shoulder and stepped into the house.

I could not describe the shock that I experienced at that moment. Such a murky and fathomless chaotic state when my soul was swirled into a whirlwind and thrown into confusion! I felt great dizziness and bumped my head on the wall. A roaring sound blew in my head. I knew what it means for the soul to depart the body.

Hyun Soo coming to the door step while carrying the clothes of J.J. turned around from the house perplexedly and hurriedly and took the clothes back to the car, as soon as he saw me burst out crying. As I saw the car carrying the clothes of J.J. leaving; I tried to stop the car. Unable to make one step further, I just crumbled to the floor. John stacked some boxes containing J.J.'s personal items in the basement, moving back and forth. When he heard me crying John silently came and hugged me. Truly J.J. is not in the world......

I could not sleep once again as I suffered a high fever and a severe head ache. I felt stiffened and was unable to move my body, as if it had hardened. Although I tried to turn to my other side, my body would not move, no matter how hard I would try. Finally, I tried to move my finger, but it was still inactive. All I could do was just sweat trying to make a move. I imagined myself dying in such a way. February 12th, 2004 Coming down to the basement, I unpacked the smallest suitcase. Various things that J.J. cherished were scattered and abandoned inside losing their value. Various CDs that he collected, some key holders he collected from his travels, precious things that J.J. was really attached to! While packing these into a box, I just collapsed, losing my spirit. The world that we happened to visit as mere humans!

What value do these things have? Silently, God guided me to draw myself near to the Scripture.

"In all your ways acknowledge him, and he will make your paths straight. (Proverbs 3:6)"

"Yes! There is no answer existing in this world. All I have to do is to have hope and to grab the Word of God who will save me." I would have to trust that God's plan for my life would not end at this point. Gradually, I could sense my heart re-opening to God again.

I could remember the Korean proverb, which is "Life is a dew on the grass," expressing the transience and fragility of life. It really described how I felt about the state of my heart.

Chapter Nine

The Consolation Coming from the Above

"The LORD is close to the brokenhearted and saves
those who are crushed in spirit (Psalm 34:18)"

February 18th, 2004 Mrs. Young Hee Jang, sent me a
note that comforted me with beautiful thoughts.
I could sense that God became the Lord of my life
and controlled my life. I also felt that I changed into the soul
gazing to God intently. My self-righteousness that had always
taken pride in me was already shattered. I just came to know
how absurd it was to set a futile plan or to desire intently.
Now could I repent of the foolishness and futility of my plan
and desire? At any rate, it was my irreversible fallacy. Reading
the Scripture all day long, I came to start to meditate on the
Scripture. As I read, "Imitation of Christ" sent by Mrs. Jang,
I humbly repent of my past full of pride against God that

happened many times a day as well as of the lowliness of my being. Moreover, I also began to understand that I exist for the sake of God, not for me.

I came to drink the Scripture as a thirsty deer drinks water. The Word was really sweet like honey. I thirsted for more and more, as I drank the Word more and more, as if I was drinking living water. The Word of God came to permeate and saturate my arid heart with grace. I felt, my heart fully filled and saturated with grace.

February 23rd 2004, I could not sleep well on account of the pain around my lower back and stiffened muscles, last night. I visited the doctor's office and got diagnosed. The doctor diagnosed that I might have a ruptured disk around my lower back and neck and stiffened muscles due to stress. He advised me to take a sedative to lessen the stress. Taking my prescriptions in a spiritless manner, I went back home.

I perceived that the stress cannot be cured by secular medicine, as stress always comes from the heart. I had a firm belief that my disease could only be healed by God's grace. I had a certainty that God would heal me some day March 1st, 2004 "Surely, he took up our infirmities and carried our sorrows, yet we considered him stricken by God, smitten by him, and afflicted. But he was pierced for our transgressions, he was crushed for our iniquities; the punishment that brought us peace was upon him, and by his wounds we are healed. We all, like sheep, have gone astray, each of us has turned to his own way; and the astray, each of us has turned to his own way; and the 6)"

How had I read the bible before without tears? I read this verse while sobbing silently. Every single word of the Scripture seemed to move like a living organism, to pierce my heart like a sword. I could sense the Holy Spirit entering my heart and breaking my ego apart. Jesus Christ, who did not forsake his people filled with sins, appeared to us in the form of a human, only to take up the sins of all the human kind and ransom their sins by being punished on the cross. I cried over and over as I was so thankful to God for his grace that never let us perish, perceiving his great love that ventured to crucify his only son for the sake of human kind. "You must have felt so painful when your only son was crucified. I confess that I dare not say that I know of even a slight portion of your suffering and love. Please forgive me, such a cruel and sinful human!"

I am only God's creature; he is really the lord of my life. I hurt him on account of my sins and I confessed my sins to him one more time with my tears. I could sense that God was also suffering with me in silence and touched me with his tender hand spiritually. It was then that I understood that the Holy Spirit was really alive and he was leading my life.

"Lord! I know that my life is shaped in your plan. Please lead my life to righteousness and transform my personality into your image! Please use me as you want, because you are my Lord who created me. I humbly wish that I could live the life that you want me to live."

Finishing this prayer, I found myself totally surrendering to God's disposal. As soon as this happened, I suddenly trusted God. I just wondered why I had not been able to do this simple thing before. As I entrusted everything to God, my mind felt peaceful. I felt liberated in the truth. I cried that night with the tears of a repenting heart, and joy in the midst of the sea of grace, thinking about his love. The next morning, I could not open my eyes right away because my eyes were swollen. I put an ice pack on my eyes. It was really a brand-new day with a radiant sun shining brightly, even though the eyes that faced this new morning were swollen like those of a frog.

March 18ᵗʰ, 2004 my constant headaches that had distressed me subsided and the symptom of insomnia gradually disappeared. At some point, I started to awake frequently while sleeping. However, I felt that I could fall asleep again easily and sleep more comfortably than previously. My stiff muscles seemed to get better. I realized that all this progress was due to my prayers and the trust I had that God will heal the disease of my body as well as of my heart. I could sense that my faith, that had almost been lost, came to be rekindled by God's grace.

March 30ᵗʰ, 2004. One of John's cousins, Cindy, was married to Gary, and they had one daughter and one son. As her daughter, Brook, was a year younger than J.J. John and I had cared and thought about Brook and her brother often. I had met Cindy once or twice. Since Cindy lived so far away, we had not seen each other often, except at the time of our wedding.

Unexpectedly, I received a card from Cindy. Cindy said that she was really shocked and distressed at the news of J.J.'s death, but unable to come to the funeral as she was traveling. She also added that our suffering was beyond her imagination, and she could only guess about the pain that we endured. She suggested that we could divert our sorrow by spending some time in a remote place. She encouraged us to come to her villa located on the island of Maui in Hawaii. She said that the natural scenic beauty of Maui would help us heal. She also sent some travel money. We really felt a great comfort and gratitude for her generosity.

I believed that Cindy was a blessed one from God because she had such a loving kindness. We could not say no to her gift because of her beautiful generosity and warm consideration.

Even though we did not have an appetite for traveling, I had some vague hope that my memories of the tragic event could be eroded and washed away if I would spend some time in such an exotic place as Maui. We replied to Cindy that we would like to go.

April 1st 2004, I was surprised as I looked at the calendar, that it was already April. Expecting that fleeting time would alleviate my suffering, I almost did not look at the calendar during those long days of winter that finally gave way to April. God took away the gloomy and dreary days of winter and brought a new season. I could not help but thank God for his grace.

"You will surely forget your trouble, recalling
it only as waters gone by" (Job 11:16).

Ruminating on this verse over and over, the conviction that God would take my sorrow away grew within me. The Lord who created me and placed such an insignificant creature in his eternal plan! It occurred to me that God was training me with his love in order to shape me into a new creature. God led me to an acknowledgment that the way to get through this test is only possible through faith and the grace of God. However, I was still struggling with my own will to repress the suffering and to overcome it, as I was still immature spiritually even though I knew the truth in my heart.

We visited J.J every week. At first, we went there together on Saturday. After that I tried to avoid visiting together, rather opting for a visit on another day during the week. It was because it was so sad and grievous for me to see John standing in front of J.J.'s tomb.

Psalm 23 was inscribed on his tombstone. I really wanted to inscribe what I would like to tell him as his mom in another way. I thought about the marble benches scattered in George Washington Memorial Park. Instead of erecting a tombstone vertically, they place a tombstone horizontally, laying it on the ground. Therefore, whoever would like to erect a vertical tombstone usually ordered a marble bench and had an epigraph inscribed on it.

We brought our plan to a tombstone dealer. It seemed that the bench for commemorating J.J. would be placed right next to the road leading to the portion of the church cemetery reserved for Yong Sang church. I wished that this bench would be used by anyone visiting the cemetery to ponder their life. We could not have many words inscribed on the marble bench, but had to make it concise and short. However, we could a have picture inscribed on both sides of the marble bench. John and I selected a picture of a cross and a dove.

On the upper part of the bench, J.J.'s name would be

inscribed. On the left side the picture of a cross would be carved, while the picture of a dove on the right side. And we had the epigraph inscribed in the middle, "We will love you and hold you in our hearts forever. God bless you! Love! Mom and Dad."

"J.J.! I love you forever until the day I will leave this world; I will bear you in my heart! Today my longing for you was so great that I am really distressed, as I meditated on the Word of God." 'The LORD is close to the brokenhearted and saves those who are crushed in spirit. (Psalm 34:18),' I received a great comfort from this verse. I was burnt with the zeal to get closer to God. It appeared that I seemed to be drawn nearer to him than before. Today I really focused on God who had been granting me great comfort.

April 13th, 2004. My body is healed every day, my spirit is also transformed. I now realized that I might enjoy further spiritual growth.

"Do not conform any longer to the pattern of this world, but be transformed by the renewing of your mind. Then you will be able to test and approve what God's will is-- his good, pleasing and perfect will. (Romans 12:2)" I carved this Word into my heart.

April 18th, 2004 people treated me and John as usual, as if they seemed to forget about J.J. Although forgetfulness might be so natural to human beings, I was bit disappointed and grieved that people weren't remembering our son.

The more forgetful people became, the more deeply attached we became to the memories of J.J. We were filled with anxieties and worries that J.J.'s friends might forget about him even though a short span of time had passed. He is not in this world any more but he was still living with us.

April 23rd 2004, I looked at the cards and letters again. I

tried to recall those to whom we felt thankful for coming to the funeral. There were some letters and cards from people that we did not know very well. One of them, was a card sent by an old couple who lived near to us but whom we had never met. I read their card with surprise.

After introducing who they were, they wrote about their story of losing their 23-year-old son. Their son had died in an accident, when he collided with a big tree on a ski trip with his close friends. They said that they could understand how we might feel and would like to help us if there would be anything that they could do. The old couple wrote such a long letter, recollecting their painful memories, in order to comfort us. I determined to visit them after reading the card. I was really hesitant about meeting them. Today, I decided to express my thankfulness to them and went outside to search for their house.

That house was located one-block away from my house. I walked over to visit their house in the evening. On the way there after several hesitations, I finally knocked on the door. An old man opened the door and I explained who I was. He welcomed me into his home. Stepping into the house, I saw a big picture of a good-looking young man hung on the wall in the living room. I thought that this young man might have been the son that they lost.

They held my hand and began to talk about the stories of their son that they lost in the ski accident 23 years ago. Their scars from the loss of their son seemed to fade away, but still remained clearly visible. I began to tell them the story of J.J. However, at last, I burst out crying, unable to control my feelings. I apologized for crying. They said that right now was the time to cry over the loss. And they also said that any time I needed to cry or talk to come to them.

Before coming out of the house of the old couple, I told them that we would meet our sons in the heaven. With unconvinced gazes, they replied back that they are not sure whether their son might recognize them, as they had gotten older. I was a bit distressed about their uncertainties. As I was not that different from them, I was concerned. I strongly urged them to have hope about the existence of heaven. In a certain sense, it was a kind of a conscious reconfirmation of my faith.

We soothed the scars of each other and felt some intimacy growing in our hearts, as if we had been close friends. Only those who experienced that pain can know the price of that pain.

Chapter Ten

The Spring Coming Again

"I lift up my eyes to the hills-- where does my help come from? My help comes from the LORD, the Maker of heaven and earth (Psalm 121:1-2)."

May 1st, 2004. Today, I arranged various pictures of J.J. and placed them into an album. I arranged the different pictures in a chronological order. I looked at how his appearance had over the years, and arranging these pictures in the album, I finally looked into a picture of the grown-up J.J.; taken with his college friends, just a month before his death. The fact that there were no more pictures of J.J. left; made me totally shocked. I tightly held that last picture for a while.

All of our life's memories were fully concentrated in each picture. As I looked into each picture, the memories of the past flowed through my mind and heart inflicting me severely with its vividness. It was different from pulsating water that just flows ceaselessly, my pain seemed to be stagnant in my memories.

May 9th, 2004 Pastor Kyung Chul Woo who was in charge of our church unit did precious pastoral care for me. I was so thankful for the comfort that the pastor gave to me. I came to have trust in his ministry. The pastor took charge of the parish that I belonged to. He served each individual member of his parish with incredible sincerity. His ministry really inspired me. I was so thankful to God for introducing me to such a good pastor. I believed that God would bless him for the rest of his life. I prayed that he would keep being a messenger of love who could keep his heart open to his lay people and share his Christian love with them.

May 12th, 2004 it was my first Mother's Day without my son. How can I describe such a feeling of loss? Obviously, I used to be a mother even a year ago. However, as there was not any son who could call me mom, I was not a mother any longer. I struggled severely with this awkwardness that I was forced to face. A Mother's Day without my son was really painful to me, reminding me of the scar that seemed to fade but was still aching.

I could recollect my son who used to do his best to surprise me, especially during this time of the year. So many funny things that he tried to plot, in order to know what I would like to receive as a present on Mother's Day! His absurd attempt to give me a homemade card that he designed, saying that he did not have enough money to buy a card! The funny contents of his awkward card made me laugh and be happy! I could not do anything all day long because his smiling face haunted my heart constantly. A Mother's Day that had been a great fun turned into an infliction that changed every happy memory into a painful recollection of the loss of my son.

Distressed, I looked out the window. Suddenly, around lunch

time, Jang-Mi, who had attended at the same school that J.J. had come to visit me with a bundle of roses, on behalf of J.J. God sent this considerate and lovely girl to me to comfort my lonely heart. My day dream that someone might visit me on Mother's Day came to be realized. I was so moved and embraced Jang Mi tightly. Sobbing, she greeted me with "Happy Mother's Day!" Jang-Mi was really mature and tender which was different from me at her age I was not as considerate as she was.

"So, in Christ we who are many forms one body, and each member belongs to all the others (Romans 12:5)."

Every moment that I needed a helping hand, God sent me different persons who filled me with the comfort that I required. I could sense that my faith was growing slowly but gradually under the guidance of the Holy Spirit. The Lord embraced me, such a weak creature, and healed me. As I thought about this, I got impatient to be a messenger who would preach the love of God.

May 20th, 2004 as I left the house, I could see an azalea bush standing bright having endured the harsh winter. The azalea that had endured the winter though an obedient attitude deeply rooted in the ground, was revealing its pink flowers that shined forth its beauty. Moreover, the green lawn that covered the front yard proudly revealed its life. Dandelions scattered in the lawn also sprouted the power of life, praising God with its leaves spreading to the sky and its pistils and stamens crowned with its flowers. It occurred to my mind that life is so enduring. I also wished to blossom like a fragrant flower which endured a harsh winter while vitally rooted firmly in the ground.

May 25th, 2004 the office that managed the cemetery, contacted us to check on the bench that they had installed for J.J. Suddenly, I supposed an opposite situation where John and

I was dead because of a car accident, leaving J.J. all alone in the world and driving him into the depth sorrows. It would have been more painful and sorrowful then what really happened. It would be better for us (his parents) to suffer those pains than for him to suffer them. The love of parents towards their child is greater than the loss of their life.

> "'For I know the plans I have for you,'
> declares the LORD, 'plans to prosper you
> and not to harm you, plans to give you
> hope and a future.'" (Jeremiah 29:11)

I meditated on this verse and hoped that God would use me for his good purpose. But I was still thankful to God that we could take care of J.J.'s final phase of life.

June 3rd, 2004 on that day, I received a call from John's brother that their mother died. She had begun to suffer from dementia 4 years ago, when John's father had died. She was always so tender to me because she did not have any daughters. She had been so kind and tender and she took care of me so considerately, whenever I visited her. She used to keep working in the kitchen making food for her children and their family, whenever we would visit her. I used to also spend time in the kitchen doing the dishes whenever we had a family reunion.

I felt so guilty about not being able to visit her more often when she spent the last days of her life in a nursing home. My heart was filled with anguish, during the long trip to Ohio for her funeral. It was reported that she died peacefully while taking a nap after eating her breakfast.

June 4th 2004, we had the funeral service at a Catholic church. This church was said to be so old in this area, that even John's mother had attended as a young child. It was said that her sisters were still attending this church. The ceiling of the church was so high. Thus, it was little bit shady and cool even in the June.

As soon as the service started, a magnificent hymn flew out of the choir with the accompaniment of a pipe organ. It resonated from the back of the church to the ceiling, hitting the empty space of the church. The hymn sung for a funeral mass seemed to have a more sorrowful tune than that of the protestant church. The priests were walking around the coffin and spreading the incense and holy water on it, repeating "from dust to dust." This phrase really hit my ears and dragged me into a kind of delusion; sedating my mind and making me shudder, with my agitated soul.

The funeral service of John's mother reminded once again of the mortality of a human. I ruminated on my past that clung to what is perishable. As it came to be the time to bid farewell to her, we could not but burst out crying. A funeral march with the smoke of incense permeating the air, without leaving any trace of its existence.

June 5th, 2004 since my mother-in-law had spent her last three years at the nursing home, unable to take care of her house, a brother of John used to manage the house. We stepped into the house after the funeral for the first time since she moved to the nursing home. Although we had visited the house numerous times, it was strange to us. Many household furnishings were scattered and dispersed around the house covered with dust. So many personal items that had been endeared by the John's mother for many years were abandoned, as if they lost any meaning as well as utility. I came to realize that those many possessions were just vacuous illusions. I concluded that I had to arrange my life and possessions. It made my heart so grieved that all those decorations that she tried to polish were full of dust.

June 10th 2004, I have thought about the question of what is the meaning of life if we lose our beloveds one by one and do not have any hope for heaven. Without the hope of heaven, the more years lived in this world did not seem to have any meaning. The question of the existence of the heaven came to be a more compelling question than any other. The many years that I spent with J.J. and John's mother just disappeared as if it had happened in a dream.

Some earthly desires to possess more "things" disappeared

gradually and the standard of my value shifted. Instead of worrying about earthly matters, I kept grappling with the question of what kind of life I should live, in order to offer the life pleasing to God. I kept envisioning the invisible heavens instead of the visible world.

June 19th, 2004 departing from Philadelphia airport at 11:30 AM, and stopping over and shifting to another plane bound for Honolulu after a 2-hour layover, John and I were finally heading toward Hawaii. The plane floating over clouds seemed to penetrate them as well as to glide over them in the bright sky. The airplane seemed to be like a glacier floating over the blue sea. When the plane descended down, lowering its altitude, I could see many roads arranged like a grid or the web of spider out the window. As I tried to see farther with slit eyes, I could see cars as small as ants going here and there.

A great city that human kind constructed was merely a small thing located in a corner of the earth, if we could see it from the view point in the sky. I could not see any other human below because of the high altitude. Once again, I could perceive that I was just an insignificant being as tiny as a grain of sand on a vast beach.

I could not but help praise the omniscience and omnipotence of God as I came to think that God was controlling every small thing, even as tiny as a grain of sand. I am a being as insignificant as a grain of sand! By thinking about that I felt smaller and smaller.

We vacationed every year during J.J.'s life. This was the first trip that I had without J.J. beside me. This travel seemed to be so futile without joy, more an escape rather than a trip.

After spending 10 hours in the airplane, we finally arrived at the Honolulu airport. We then shifted to a smaller airplane and headed to Maui. The plane glided over the sea flashing with light reflecting the sun, like a silver plate.

Cirrus clouds were scattered all over the place above the horizon where the sky and the sea were converging. It seemed that the peace of God covered this place. I also dispersed my crystallized sorrow like those clouds. I felt freed, sensing that my aching heart got scattered and dispersed among those clouds. After 30 minutes, we arrived at Maui. As soon as we landed at the airport, we went to the rental car service where we had a reservation and rented a car. Driving for around 40 minutes, we arrived at Wailea Point where Cindy's villa was located. As I entered Wailea Point, I could see many beautiful villas surrounded with beautiful flowers and a fantastic beach. I could not but describe this place as a paradise.

Many hotels were scattered in the district near Wailea Point. Cindy's house was surrounded with a beautiful garden. At the entrance leading to Cindy's house, there were some security guards keeping watch at the gate. After certifying our identities, they opened the gate and let us drive to the house. Except for some workers who were busy managing the gardens filled with various tropical plants and flowers, I could not see anyone who seemed to reside in that neighborhood. I saw a scene of the sea enfolding between great palm trees. We could only exclaim "Wow!"

Upon entering the house, we viewed the house itself as a piece of art so beautiful that you could tell it was designed by a special interior designer. Tables, chairs, couches, and decorations were well organized and harmonious. I could sense the exquisite taste of the owner of this house. One side wall had some buttons so I pressed one of them, suddenly the curtain which hung over a very large window rolled up and revealed a beautiful scene of the sea. It was such a beautiful scene that it could have appeared in a movie. Next to the window there were two arm chairs. Between them, there was a table with a sculpture in the form of a sail boat placed on it.

The sculpture was so wonderful in that it looked like a transparent sail boat floating over the blue sea reflecting the sun light. Whenever I had some time, I sat next to that sculpture, letting all those senses of the loss, pains and sufferings flow toward that vast ocean. Loading those pains on that transparent sail boat and making them float over the sea. I was really thankful to God for granting such a wonderful time in my life.

June, 20th, 2004 we left the villa to take a group tour. Everywhere we went in Maui we could see the Haleakala Volcano. Our tour was going to take us around the Haleakala Volcano. It was a beautiful scene of a volcanic mountain surrounded with clouds in the middle and tinged with cobalt blue and green. The scene of clouds floating around the top of the cobalt blue mountain inspired inexpressible feeling as if I was in an ancient time.

The trip was supposed to consist of following a narrow mountain track around the mountain side of Haleakala volcano. We would visit a village called Hana. Hana is the Hawaiian word for flower. We saw flowers everywhere in Maui. The tourist bus began by making a spiral climb on the mountain side with great skilled effort. On the hillside, the road came to be craggier as well as narrower. At one point, the road was so narrow that one car needed to wait until the other coming toward it could pass by.

According to what the tour guide said, a landslide can happen when it rains and it could obstruct the road. In that case, he said that trees or soils would have to be cleared if it obstructs the road. He said that there could be a delay if there was a land side. He added that we should enjoy the tour because the weather on this day was perfect. It seemed that scenes of Haleakala's mysterious primeval forest with wild flowers tinged with innumerable colors, plants and trees covering jungles, fragile reeds sprouting out of crags and rocks, were suggestive of the beauty of heaven.

The road that was paved around the sea was situated beside a cliff so steep that I could not dare look out. As I look out the window, I could see a deep blue sea opening its mouth hundreds of feet below. I noticed a small wild flower rooted and almost unnoticeable beyond the attention of people, fulfilling its duty blossoming there. I still pondered on the preciousness of life. If God would never neglect even a small wild flower, he would not neglect me. The garden of God! I could see a hillside seen from the distance shrouded with flowers. "Yes! I should live in order to be obedient to God for Him as well as for His calling, just like that small wild flower. I pushed my head back toward the sky and looked higher and higher as I ascended higher and higher. Then I closed my eyes.

Then, I gazed up at God. The love of God pulsated and then fluctuated in my heart. My body was trembling with this impression, feeling Gods presence in me. I raised my arms high and praised God. Tears ran down my face ceaselessly. In the midst of Haleakala Mountain, the garden of God shrouded with flowers, I could feel the hope for the heaven growing gradually as well as definitely.

The Hana Village was located on the hillside and retained its pristine beauty, insulated from any trace of civilization. It was said that there were native Hawaiians who followed their old customs. Moreover, there was another village located in a higher hillside more isolated than Hana, having neither electricity nor a hospital. It is said that they apply herbal treatment to an illness, following their traditional medicines. Although they had been resisting being civilized as well as refusing contact with the outside, they were said to be happier than anyone else. On the other hand, I could see some villas constructed in the side of the mountain overlooking the sea. Ironically, the village of native Hawaiians refusing to be affiliated into civilization and persisting in living in poverty seemed to be quite harmonized with the villas of the affluent people.

Coming down from the mountain, the driver stopped the bus on a plain filled with tropical plants. Looking down to the one side, I could see the deep blue sea. Following down to the other side, I found a beach spreading in the form of semi-circle. On the beach covered with black sand, waves were rolling and bubbling foam as well as roaring against rocks breaking the silence. A young couple, who were on the same bus, were having a fun time, taking pictures. I smiled faintly, recollecting that I used to have such a wonderful time in my life. As I look over the sea spreading infinitely sitting on a rock, I was seized with the sense of futility of mortal beings.

As I climbed over a hill, I saw a small chapel standing on it. According to the tour guide, some people would gather and worship in this chapel once a month. He said that a pastor would come for this infrequent worship service. I saw John coming out of the chapel through reeds and bushes. He said that he went to the chapel, prayed for a while, and donated some money. There was a small cemetery next to the chapel. Some tombstones that looked old, witnessing its long history, stood alone, revealing that how those who are buried in that cemetery had a lonely end to their lives. I was being seized with the sense of loneliness, as I look at those tombstones that came to be worn by rains and winds, without having any trace of human contact for a long time. I felt so certain that all mortal humans are nothing but creatures that would eventually turn to ash. I was standing there, intermingled with those unidentifiable flowers and plants. It seemed that these creatures filled with life were praising God, keeping their own unique place on the hill revealing their best looks in harmony with the sound of waves. I also praised God for those plants and flowers, imagining myself as a part of nature, like a small flower, attributing praise to God, who controls the universe.

"O Lord! You are the potter. I am thankful to you for making my gaze directed to you through the long processes of pains and sufferings. I am also thankful for your refining me through these hardships. Please do not discard me. Please use me as your vessel. I truly believe that those sufferings and tribulations will be healed and recovered under the great plan of your providence. I truly believe that you will lead me to the best. I really thank you that you revealed your great love to me, such an insignificant human."

"I lift up my eyes to the hills-- where does my help come from? My help comes from the LORD, the Maker of heaven and earth." (Psalm 121:1-2) This verse just lingered in my mind, on the way back to the villa.

June 21st, 2004 as it was said that the sunrise seen from the top of Haleakala volcano is world famous, we decided to see it, in spite of burdens of waking up at 2 AM. As we had to depart around 2 AM, I tried to go to bed early. However, I could not fall asleep. Waking up after the several hours of insomnia, I saw a travel bus waiting for us at front of the gate. Most of the tour guides were native Hawaiians. They seemed to work with sense of pride and contribution, looking younger than they were. A female driver, who was also in her sixties, drove the bus quite deftly, telling her story. She said, that she visited her home once a week. She had nine siblings who all lived quite close in the neighborhood. She said that she felt most comfortable living in her home located on the high hill side, although there was no electricity as well as any trace of civilization. Her remark that she was thankful to God for letting her be born in that place was really moving. It made such a contrast with those modern people who forget to be thankful to God in spite of the full benefits from civilization. According to what she said, Maui had been changed a lot. She said that it was bit painful to see the natural area being developed and finally losing its pristine life. I totally agreed with her remark that there is nothing better than nature.

That small bus visited every hotel where its passengers were waiting for them. Then, it stopped in front of a restaurant and the passengers got off the bus; where we transferred to a bigger bus which was waiting for us. The bus began to move slowly after every passenger got on. The bus driver advised passengers to take a nap for an hour until it reached the top of mountain. He turned off all the lights of the bus. After many people moved around in their seats to find the most comfortable posture for having a nap, it became quiet. Hearing the engine roaring as it climbed on a slant, I fell asleep and took a nap until the bus arrived at the top of the mountain.

Arriving at the top of the mountain, I could see many buses unloading people desiring to see the sun rise on the top of Haleakala. It is not dawn yet and still dark. There were lights only on the observation platform as well as in a souvenir kiosk. With the observation platform being located in the middle, there was a low wall with a railing surrounding it, so that people in a circle could see the sun rising.

As I grabbed the railing and looked down, I felt dizziness at such a precipitous cliff. As I looked into the cliff carefully, various craters are laid out mysteriously as well as infinitely, forbidding the access by humans, thus maintaining its primordial condition, and revealing its innumerable ages. The surface inside the craters seemed be to be delicate. It seemed that my one step would crumble the entire surface into its fathomless pit. It looked so tender and smooth, as if covered with some dust. It reminded me of the surface of Mars and the moon, with different colors all around. Standing against the wind on the top of the mountain in serenity, I felt like I was in some other world. Everyone was facing eastwards, expecting the sun to rise. A woman selling souvenirs at the kiosk suddenly jumped up on the parapet. It was such a dangerous move that may lead her to fall off the cliff. It frightened me. That woman sitting on the parapet looking like a sturdy man shouted some spells toward the sky. It seemed that she was performing some kind of a rite. Her shouts were echoed back against the side of the mountain.

A few minutes later, the sun was rose, around 4:45 A.M. As the sun was rising, it was dyeing everything with its yellow, orange and red rays and shining forth its light. The light was so intense and dazzling that I could not open my eyes. Many people waiting for the sunrise began to exclaim simultaneously, WOW! As the sun was rising with its magnificence and majesty and dyeing the sky with its light, many people remained silent watching over the ever-changing panorama of lights taking place in the sky with its dazzling variations every second. Watching those magnificent and majestic scenes, I tried to imagine the moment of God's creation that might break the silence of the primordial world. Once again, I could not but feel the hand of God on the top of Haleakala!

> "Yours, O LORD, is the greatness and the
> power and the glory and the majesty and the
> splendor, for everything in heaven and earth is
> yours. Yours, O LORD, is the kingdom; you are
> exalted as head over all." (1 Chronicles 29:11)

Chapter Eleven

The Embrace in a Dream

"You will seek me and find me when you seek me with all your heart. (Jeremiah 29:13)" July 1st, 2004.

I woke up from the deep sleep that I had from the long journey, everything that I enjoyed in Maui seemed to be a dream. As soon as we woke up, we prepared ourselves to go out, to see J.J. John went out of the house with a bottle filled with fresh water. We bought a bundle of flowers at a flower shop before entering the cemetery. John was taking the lead, with a bottle of water. I was following him with a bundle of flowers. The sky was so clear; the hill was so beautiful, covered with green grass, at the time when the heat of noon did not begin yet. I stepped one by one with such a grave heart. Although coming back from such a wonderful trip, the sorrow in my heart did not seem to go away entirely, my heart still felt heavy.

John buried a small volcanic stone that he brought from Maui. He buried it right next to the tombstone. J.J had collected small stones when he was little and this was another one for him. "If you had been there, you definitely would have picked up such a stone. So, I picked one on behalf of you. J.J., I love you. I really miss you!" John was sobbing slightly. I sighed, crying "Oh God!" "Oh God!"

We read the 23rd Psalm slowly. "The LORD is my shepherd; I shall not be in want. He makes me lie down in green pastures, he leads me beside quiet waters, he restores my soul. He guides me in paths of righteousness for his name's sake. Even though I walk through the valley of the shadow of death, I will fear no evil, for you are with me; your rod and your staff, they comfort me. You prepare a table before me in the presence of my enemies. You anoint my head with oil; my cup overflows. Surely goodness and love will follow me all the days of my life, and I will dwell in the house of the LORD forever." (Psalm 23) After reading this passage, we then recited the Lord's Prayer, choking with tears.

July 10th, 2004. Today, I sent a thank-you card to Cindy. "Dear Cynthia! We are still very sad. It has been really difficult living without J.J. He was our life, our dreams, and our hope. Some mornings, I wake up and still cannot believe he is gone. There have been our friends, people like you that help us heal our broken hearts and souls. While we were in Hana, we saw numerous kinds of beautiful flowers which of I cannot remember their names. But they were so wonderful and attractive that I told myself Heaven should be much better, and it gave me reassurance that J.J. is in a better place. I prayed on the mountain, "God give us a beautiful mind like Cynthia, so that we can share lots of love with many people and help others who are also suffering." I can't say thank you enough. God Bless You... Love, Karen."

July 26th, 2004 a group of J.J.'s friends, whom J.J. used to meet every summer, visited us. I had wished that J.J.'s friends would visit us. As it turned out, my wish came true. It was such a wonderful joy to think that they thought of us. We felt as if we were now seeing our son again. More than anything else, their warm and tender consideration was really moving. They seemed to be the ones who were embedded in our hearts, filling the absence of our son. I really would like to keep in touch with them, as we felt still connected to J.J. through the ties with J.J.'s friends. We were so thankful that they suggested first that they would keep in touch with us. We could not conceal our thoughts and desire to hear anything related to J.J. John, Jimmy H, Jimmy W, Tommy, Danny, and Mark visited us. I gave them some money to have a party in J.J.s honor. Before coming back, they said that they would visit the place where J.J. was buried. We were so thankful for their remarks and they gave so much comfort to us.

July 30th, 2004. I wrote a letter to J.J. J.J! I was at a loss of how to observe your birthday after thinking about it all day. As I had no idea of how to commemorate it, I wished that I had been able to avoid the day. However, time was so cruel that it woke up my soul and pushed me to confront the day. Yes. Today, July 30th, is your 21st birthday! Oh, My Son! The world without your presence is so desolate and empty. I really miss your hearty laugh that made me forget about all my worries. If I watch a home video, I can see you and hear your voice. However, I am still not prepared for it. Maybe, as time goes by someday, I might be able to watch it. You were the most precious treasure that God endowed us. You may not imagine how happy we were because of you. When you went away to college, we had to confront a temporary separation. Without having any experience of separation from you for 18 years, I felt some sense of loss at that time. While dropping you in front of the dorm, I seemed to sense the pain of separation imposed as a destiny for every human. I did not expect that the separation from you might be permanent and so soon.

As I left the dorm with a fast pace in order to conceal my tears, I could sense your compassionate gaze behind my back. You were so compassionate and warm that you would share your tenderness with many people that you met. On the way home from the dorm, the sun was setting, stretches of the sky and ridges of the mountains were streaked with red. As I was looking at the twilight, your father and I were just gazing at the sky, feeling a sense of loneliness and futility. At that time, there was a bird soaring toward the intensely glaring sunset. I thought of you as I was seeing that lonely bird, thinking that you would have to soar higher and higher into your own dream, your future and destiny, departing from the bosom of your parents.

It seems that you soared too high and too early into the heaven! Oh, my son, the time here in this temporal world is just fleeting and transient like a short dream. I will soar into heaven where you stay with inexpressible joy, when my spirit departs from my body. Until then, I will live faithfully to my calling while I am in this world within the span of time that God grants to me. I will soar higher and higher filled with brimming joy into heaven with an intense hope that I will stay with you and God eternally. When we meet in heaven let's not separate any more. If we hold hands tightly and we never let go we will always be together.

> "He will wipe every tear from their eyes.
> There will be no more death or mourning

or crying or pain, for the old order of things
has passed away. (Revelation 21:4).”

August 1ˢᵗ, 2004. I had an American friend named Carletta. She was married to a Korean man Jong Soo Sohn. She could cook more kinds of Korean food then I could. Sometimes, I was confused who might be the real Korean, Carletta or me. Carletta and Jong Soo once adopted a baby from Korea. He was a baby 10 months old. Sadly, this baby suddenly passed away two months after the adoption. She said that they had a really hard time, on account of their shock at the death of their son. Their sharing of their experience really gave me great comfort.

Carletta said that she could not sleep after her baby died and overcoming the grief was difficult. What made them grievous above all was the uncertainty whether the baby would go to the heaven or not. She prayed to God every day that God would reveal the truth concerning whether the baby went to the heaven, as she believes that God's revelation of the destiny of the baby might alleviate her grief. One day, she could see the baby embraced by his parents in her dream. From that time on, she felt a bit relieved at her loss. She also added that God would reveal that J.J.'s was in the heaven in my dream, if I would pray more sincerely.

“But those who hope in the LORD will renew
their strength. They will soar on wings like
eagles; they will run and not grow weary; they
will walk and not be faint.” (Isaiah 40:31)

August 3ʳᵈ, 2004 wishing to see J.J. even once in my dream, I kept thinking of him before I slept. Sometimes, I tried to be obsessed with the thinking of J.J. all day long. I tried to do my best so that I could meet him in my dream, strangely, I could not dream about J.J. for seven months. Usually, I would dream of something that could not be understood in reality I began to pray to God to show me that J.J. was in heaven and would appear in my dream. I still could not see him for several months. I really got nervous and felt unrewarded. Moreover, I felt stupid as I was requesting such a thing sought from the unbelief of heaven. I did not give up. I kept praying to God as I was so certain that God would answer me for sure, if it is really necessary for me. I kept praying constantly.

August 5th, 2004 the dream was clear and it was so fantastic that I could remember everything, as soon as I woke up! I offered a prayer of thankfulness to God with a trembling joy who had answered my prayer, recollecting the dream of the night. J.J. finally appeared in my dream. In the dream, there was sun light coming through the window in the afternoon. Suddenly, the door opened and J.J. stepped into the house, greeting me "Hi Mom," with his right hand raised and having a bright smile around his face. It was so clear and real that I even doubt whether it may be a dream or not. I was so glad to see him and very surprised. We embraced each other enthusiastically. It was such an ecstatic joyful feeling that I had never experienced before. It was such rapture that I could not compare it with any other experience. Embracing him, I kissed him all around his face. My son whom I had not embraced for so many months! I could not describe those mysterious and ecstatic feelings that my whole body was quivering in response to. The feeling of peacefulness was as vivid as the feeling of the warmth of his body.

That dream changed me into another person completely.

The word happiness that had no meaning to me since J.J.'s death came to be the word that could characterize my feeling. The dream really inspired hope in my heart. I was so happy that I could remember that dream so vividly all day long. I could not conceal my excitement chattering constantly, while I was bit cautious of not shattering this dream. I closed my eyes and tried to envision that dream in my mind. I could remember scene by scene. His warmth as well as the peacefulness surrounding me and J.J.......

As I experienced such a vivid dream, I could not distinguish whether it was a dream or reality. I came to have a hope that I could meet him in a dream occasionally before I could meet him in the heaven. This hope was a great comfort in return. God implanted the really firm certainty in my mind suffering my weak faith that J.J. was staying in the heaven. As I came to have a certainty concerning the existence of heaven, I came to feel a sense of attachment to the earthly life growing in me, in contrast with my previous thoughts that I would be cut off from those attachments. I came to understand that the rest of my days in this earthly life should be subservient for the preparation of entering heaven. I realized that each single moment should not be dismissed. I could sense that the gate of my heart which had been closed against the future seemed to be open toward the tomorrow. I was really thankful to God for inspiring the dream to such a foolish human who sought for any signs. I could keep the wonderful feeling aroused by that dream in my heart for some days, being enraptured with it.

August 12th, 2004. I also dreamed of a strange dream yesterday. It was night in the dream, suddenly, a flying object, shining forth its light from all of its sides hovered over my head. At that time, I felt that it must be the Lord hovering over me.

Remembering the stories of a woman suffering hemophilia, I touched that object with an expectation that my intense faith would be rewarded just as that woman's was. I was electrified with such a peaceful feeling of contentment that I felt when I embraced J.J. in my dream a week ago. It was such a feeling that some peaceful contentment was streaming into my heart, an enrapturing and mysterious feeling beyond the description of human language. As I think of the feeling of that dream, I spent all day with such a peaceful contentment, ruminating on that dream. I was so enraptured with that feeling that I enjoyed in the dream. It was intense enough to illicit smiles all day long, I had a difficulty in concealing my smile.

Although these were two different dreams, I couldn't simply dismiss them as mere dreams. It is because the feeling that these dissimilar dreams elicited were the same. I just kept these dreams to myself and did not tell anyone of them. I felt that my enduring doubt about the existence of heaven seemed to be resolved. I no longer was inflicted with this frustrating doubt. I came to realize that the heaven, that I had strived for was a superficial feeling and was already realized in my heart. I felt liberated from all of life's complications and frustrations. As I felt certain again that God had mercy on me by pouring the certainty of the heaven into my heart, I felt so grateful for God's infinite mercy and grace. I just offered the prayer of thankfulness to God, who showed me his hands of mercifulness. The joy that I had forgotten for a long time seemed to cover my entire being, once again. The heaven that I had strived to find was already embedded in my heart. Thence, I came to feel a strong attachment to my life and a willingness to embrace it which I had abandoned with despair in the past. Lying, on the bed, I tried to fall asleep. I felt inspired as I thought of what

God would prepare for me on another day.

August, 25ᵗʰ, 2004. I dreamed of another dream similar to the previous ones. In this dream, J.J. also appeared. Although each dream has a little bit of a different story, they were the same in that they inspired the same feeling in me. I was so amazed by what happened in my dreams. I could not but feel from the deepest part of my heart. I perceived that "God made me to savor the taste of the heaven in advance." I was so certain that God brought some message to me by those dreams. I also became sure that God's mercifulness brought God to reveal himself in my dream as well as in me who had the slightest faith. "Jesus came to me." Coming in the form of this beloved son, God implanted hope and comfort as well as the certainty of the heaven in my heart.

The mysteriously peaceful contentment that surrounded my whole being! That peculiar experience that I had never experienced in my earthly life seemed to belong of heaven, not to this earth. I tried to do my best to describe that feeling that is beyond the description of human language. At last, I failed to describe it and I gave up expressing it in my own words. It is because the heaven is far beyond the human imagination, thus only known by God as a secret covered against human knowledge. I felt filled with the Holy Spirit like being baptized with the fire of the Holy Spirit. I was quivering with the joy that no one might understand, with my mouth gaping with sacred delights. "You will seek me and find me when you seek me with all your heart (Jeremiah 29:13)."

Spreading over the Wings

Chapter Twelve

Sympathy of Those who are in the Same Shoes

"If one part suffers, every part suffers
with it; if one part is honored, every part
rejoices with it (1 Corinthians 12:26)."

September 11th, 2004, we visited an association called "Compassionate Friends." This association had its meeting once a month at a local Church. It was an association for helping and cheering bereft parents who had lost their children. As I entered the church, I could see some people hugging and welcoming each other as if they had known each other for a long time. They gathered by twos and threes, drinking tea or coffee and conversing with each other. It seemed that people got to know each other so easily if they had some contact point that they could share the same interests. I really felt tied to them just on the basis of my perception that we are in the same shoes.

One thing surprised me was that there were many more participants than I expected. One of the participants put some cakes and coffee on the round table, saying that it was the birthday of her son. In the middle of the room, there was a table on which were stacked various books by people having overcome the loss of their family members as well as some pastor's books. At 8 o'clock, people were grouped into two; one group was for new comers and the other consisted of the existing participants. John and I entered the room with the first group, the group of newcomers. There was a big table in the middle of the room. Many chairs were arranged around the table. As I counted the number of participants, there were 11 including us. Every participant introduced himself/herself to each other, as well as the name and the story of his/her own children that they lost.

At first, a woman named Carol began the conversation. Her son lost his life on the way home from his college in a car accident, in December, 7 years ago. She said that she could not overcome the shock and that she had been bedridden every December since. She said that she even got some psychiatric treatments. She also said that she came to participate in this program as her friend advised her to come. The thing that she said to be the most unbearable was that people around her wanted her to be the same as usual. She sobbed, saying that people just did not understand that she would never be the same as before. I could understand how she felt. Actually, we could sympathize with her as it was the story that we had also experienced. Everyone began to weep with Carol. Then, an old couple sitting next to me said that they lost their son and daughter in law in a car accident. They had a car accident on the way to a hospital to visit their friend. They also were sobbing, while saying that they were rearing two grandchildren. We just continued sobbing once again wiping our tears with some tissues.

An African American woman said that her son had been shot by one of his neighbor's rights before having an Easter dinner. She confessed that she could not repress anger from that time on. What was distressing the woman more was that people just assumed her son to be killed on account of selling drugs, although he did not have any connection with drug dealers. We just kept weeping over and over, using up tissues. Another couple, who sat in front of us keeping silent, told a shocking story. She said that she had three children, one of which had been a drug-addict. They had to go the police department to bail out their son virtually every Christmas Eve. Even in some rare case that they did not have to go to the police department, he also caused some uproars and fights among the family members. They said that it was really difficult for them to have a calm Christmas Eve. However, after their son died, they said that they could not hold any party as they so missed that son who always had caused problems so much, although they could have a relatively calm Christmas party without him. That couple kept wiping off their tears. Still, I could ascertain how deep and desperate is the love of the parents to their children. All the 11 persons staying in the room exposed their wounds to each other and shared their sufferings. We could feel those pains of each other.

When it was my turn, I told them my story. Then I said: "I just realized that my hurt could not get recovered in a human way, no matter how hard I tried. Only the word of God and the love of God can cure us. We have to live with our hope, abiding by the grace of God. Unintentionally, I preached something with certainty. At that moment, I felt the hand of the Lord healing my wounds. As we were saying goodbye to each other at the last moment of the meeting, I felt that those people who had been strange to each other got very intimate to each other, forming a community of the same destiny, like a group on board of the same ship. We were not sure of what kind of storm this vessel might confront. However, I thought that we could encourage and cheer each other when each of us gets weary, as all of us know the destination. I wanted to be a supportive power to each of us.

September 18th, 2004, I received a brochure containing some information about the children I decided to support through the organization World Vision. One of them was living with his grandmother in Cambodia; the other was staying with a distant relative like an orphan. Sometimes, I would look at their pictures, praying for them that they would grow up to belong to the people of God. I decided to support as many children as I could in such a way. I thought that they were all the children of God just as I and J.J. were.

October 17th, 2004. I knew a dentist whose name is Jin Ho Park. He was a very beautiful Christian having a gentle smile and he revealed the suggestion of Christ in his life, as he devoted himself on some medical mission trips in the midst of his busy life. Moreover, he was also a member of my music lover's association. We had frequent meetings enjoying music. I came to know that he was extremely excited about the Korean singer Duk Gyu Hah. I was also fond of that singer. However, I could not compete with Mr. Park in the interest for Hah. He said that he was really influenced by the songs of Hah when he had been struggling with his pains and sufferings during his life.

Our group initiated and planned a concert by Duk Gyu Hah. Mr. Park did his best to invite Duk Gyu Hah to Philadelphia. Finally, hah came to Philadelphia for a concert. With excited expectation, I came to listen to his music at the concert. Duk Gyu Hah confessed that he encountered God when he was wandering hopelessly at a deadlock in his life. Then, he sang a song of praise to God who had saved him and brought a new life filled with a light and a hope to him. As I knew, God whom he once had met in his suffering, I was totally immersed in his praises and confessions, full of tears. I also praised God with my whole heart.

Finally, many people at the concert sang some children's songs together, as if we had become children again. I seemed to feel some warm nostalgia as if I had met an old friend. I could see that many people were talking with each other after the concert, still being attached to the nostalgic atmosphere and hesitating to part from their friends. Different from the chilly weather, the church where the concert took place was filled with the warmth of people loving and caring for each other. After the concert, some people gathered at Min Ho Park's house. He always was willing to open his place with hospitality and generosity. There I met Mr. Duk Gyu Hah in person for the first time. I was really impressed with his gentle humility as well as his heart for all those marginalized.

October 20th, 2004. I came to learn the basic motif of the Scriptures in a systematic way during the bible study with the wife of Pastor Woo. As I studied the Scripture more and more, I came to perceive various subjects such as the assurance of salvation, life overcoming temptations, life obeying the word of God, and the life doing ministries. Therefore, I came to perceive the direction that I had to take. Moreover, I received an inexpressible grace through intercessory prayers with her. The life of Mrs. Woo, which was fully devoted to her ministries with the gift of gentleness endowed from God, was so beautiful. Mrs. Woo would pray to God that I would have many spiritual children. I was so touched with that prayer that I began to intensely pray for the children around me as well as the children of missionaries, all around the world. As in her prayer, I wanted to have as many spiritual children as I could. Day by day, the moment that I knelt communicating with God through prayer got longer and longer. This time would be the happiest moment of my daily routine.

October 29th, 2004. I received a parcel from Mr. Park. As I opened the parcel, I could see the picture of me and Duk Gyu Hah set in a beautiful frame. I was so thankful for his consideration. I regarded him as a blessed person whose heart was filled with compassion and mercy toward others. I decided to be a person who could reveal the fragrance of the Christ by providing kindness to others. I determined to provide more love to more people.

December 18th, 2004. Eileen said that the Pearl Buck Foundation that she worked for was hosting a Christmas party for the children adopted through them, I was willing to participate in the party. Jim was driving on the road leading through desolate suburban areas, filled with the dense fog. The car was passing through the darkness created by the dense fog that seemed to alternate between appearing and disappearing capriciously. Getting through the dense fog and groping though the narrow path covered with darkness, we finally arrived at the Pearl Buck Foundation.

The Foundation was located right next to the house where Pearl Buck used to live. Every detail that Pearl Buck might have arranged was preserved perfectly. The house that Pearl Buck used to live in was a big farm house. I could see various things displayed neatly, such as her typewriter, the pictures of her adopted children, Chinese collections, and the photo of her receiving the Nobel Prize in Literature. It was said that she usually wrote downstairs. I saw her typewriters and pens displayed in the room where she wrote her books. According to the explanation of the guide, Buck was a woman of discipline and self-control, she went to her office located downstairs in the morning and came out of the office only in the evening.

As I stepped into the place where the party was taking place, I could see two or three children coming in. There was even a baby. It seemed that most of them were from Asian countries. Pointing to one child, Eileen said that he was from Korea. He just looked at me as if he was doing so just because I was also an Asian. I felt so much pity for that child coming from that another county to find new parents. I tried not to show my emotions, doing my best keep back my tears. The faces of those children coming with their new parents were full of happiness. I wished that all the adoptees could set new roots and grow strongly in this country.

December 24th, 2004 it was Christmas Eve so I was thinking of J. J. I could not get over my depression today, as the memory of J.J. was really haunting my mind. Outside it was grey dark and cloudy ominously threatening rain. My heart was also filled with dark clouds as if those clouds and this bad weather had been thrust into my heart. The dark clouds slowly became rain drops in my heart. The pouring rain made a roaring sound beating onto my heart. It kept pounding ceaselessly on my heart. Kept pounding onto my heart…. Quite frequently at this time of year, John, I, and J.J used to sit on the couch, staring at the Christmas tree filled with Christmas gifts, chatting about things that we had not shared for a long time. I felt a strong sense of loss concerning various tiny moments of happiness that I could not regain. When J.J. would tell us funny things having taken place in the school, I could not but laugh all over again. Around 8 o'clock, we used to go to church to attend the Christmas Eve service, taking a candle with our hands, celebrating the coming of the baby Jesus to this world, singing Silent Night and coming out of the church with deep religious impressions. However, we were very reluctant to attend a Christmas Eve service without J.J.

We decided not to decorate a Christmas tree. Rather, it would be more correct to say that we could not. I just could not get free from my memories of the last Christmas when J.J. had been suffering in the hospital. I was so distressed, as I could not give a present to J.J. any longer. We were just agonizing over what to do, thinking about taking a trip like an escape. Suddenly, I happen to think about our friend Carol who might have been alone. As I called her, she said that she would just keep staying at home, instead of visiting the house of her brother. Hurriedly, I bought some lunch for her and headed to her house. She welcomed us so gladly. As we ate lunch together and spent the day, we felt comforted by each other. As we were trying to leave, she just approached and hugged me, with her eyes brimmed with tears. God just poured out love to me so that I could share this love with her. Also embracing her tightly, I was thankful to God for using me to comfort her. My eyes were moist like dew. On the way home from the church after Christmas Eve worship, I saw every house adorned with Christmas lights and decorations, reflecting that every family member of each house would be gathered together. I felt some loneliness in comparison with the cheer flowing out of those houses. I also thought that it was truly the night when blessings could come to this world.

December 28th, 2004 facing toward the grandiose sun rays coming through branches of a tree, I tried to stand firm like the sturdy tree that withstands winter storms. The weight of the time of the last year seemed to be longer than that the span of all those years of this tree's life. I could see some branches scattered all around the yard, fallen from the tree because of a strong wind. I deeply breathed in the fresh air of winter, as it was so refreshing to my nose and a sense of reverence to life just grew in me. I also felt the grace of God springing from my heart, He so much loved a weak creature like me and without his grace which made me sustain this life, He saved me from the miserable condition where I might have been abandoned like the twigs scattered in this yard. I still could remember the infinite bosom of the Holy Spirit who healed my despair with his enduring love, He came to me and re-built my broken heart. I also could not forget the many people who provided me hands of support so that I could stand firm again. They were the essence of Christ that led me to the light.

> "If one part suffers, every part suffers
> with it; if one part is honored, every part
> rejoices with it (1 Corinthians 12:26)."

I really would like to whisper to those who happened to make eye contact with me as well as to all those who passed by me with this: "Please give some portion of your love to your neighbors who suffer illness and loneliness. We are just one, a small member of a one body in Christ; your small concern and care can give life to those who are suffering.

December 30th, 2004 I just happened to drop by a coffee shop. I could see many people in a line conversing with each other cheerfully and with smiling faces. It seemed that many people in the world had made joyous plans that might make them happy. I felt myself isolated from their cheerfulness. I just happened to remember the day when I had to say good bye to J.J. in the hospital. I tried to put these memories out of my head, only to find that I kept thinking of them. I wished I could be in some land of oblivion if there was any. I could not erase my yearning for him although I knew that J.J. was staying well in the heaven where there would not be any suffering. My heart which was filled with a yearning for J.J. could not be satisfied by anything. I just looked at the sky and tried to calm down and still my anguish. John seemed to pretend that everything was normal sitting on a chair in front of a computer like a stone without making any move. The holiday season isolated those who are lonely with so much cruelty.

Tomorrow is the Eve of New Year's Day and is one of the most important holidays in American custom. Many people would greet the New Year by shouting and shooting off fire crackers, when the clock in Times Square in Manhattan pointed to midnight. John, I, and J.J. used to greet the New Year at church or in our home peacefully. At the first moment of New Year, we would embrace each other and pray that God's grace would remain in the life of each of us with thankfulness to God who provided us with one more year.

Chapter Thirteen

The Visit to Korea

"Blessed are the poor in spirit, for theirs is
the kingdom of heaven (Matthew 5:3)."

January 1st, 2005 preparing a traditional Korean dish for New Year's Day, I felt disturbed, as the memories of J.J. kept haunting in my mind. I tried to overcome that feeling by making myself preoccupied with treating guests. I had invited some young adults from church to my house, whose parents were still in Korea. I was really thankful for their willingness to come to my house suggesting their good will to ease the loneliness of John and me.

It was really cheerfully boisterous as people were eating and chatting with each other. However, when they returned to their home, my house was once again shrouded with a grave silence. I just washed dishes; then I turned on the T.V. lying on the couch. I could see some idyllic scene of a forest and a valley in a South American country broadcasted on T.V. It reminded me of the valley of Oui Dong near my home town, where I used to visit and play as a child. Suddenly the memory of the valley of Oui Dong in my childhood flashed in my mind so vividly. A small mountain was located between Oui Dong valley and my hometown, "Bang Hak Dong. We had to take a tour around that mountain area or to take a short cut through it, by walking for a couple of hours.

As we were just kids, we used to walk through the mountain area, which a lot of fun. We would go to Oui Dong once or twice every summer. Traveling around in a group, we used to climb up the hill for an hour chatting with each other. Then, we could take an unpaved road for a while, totally covered with dust. If we just followed that track, we found the valley of Oui Dong surrounded by a lush forest. We could also view a fresh brook running through the forest which covered the valley. Following along the valley, we saw a dark forest coming into view and the sound of the babbling brook with clear running water was music to our ears. We would swim and splash in the flowing water of the brook, unaware of the passage of time. There was a big rock on which several kids could lie together. As it had been heated up by the sun light, it was a really good place for us to warm our bodies chilled from swimming. While looking down to the bottom of a brook, I could see some pebbles and minnows swimming around here and there that tried to escape the hands of the kids trying to catch them. We used to catch them and put them in some bottles to take back home. I missed the soil of my home town where I used to play in my childhood. I wanted to go back and visit my home town and regain my strength again. I wanted to refill my memories with those beautiful scenes of my home land as vividly as I could. I missed Korea to which I hadn't been back to for 21 years. I decided to visit Korea this upcoming spring, which was bit earlier that I had originally planned.

January 15th, 2005 Caitlin made a request from the adoption agency that handled her adoption to get a photo of her birth parents. Eileen said that her birth mother wrote a letter and sent it with some photos of her family. Eileen asked me to translate it into English. The letter was full of the stories of the mother seeking forgiveness for abandoning her daughter. Moreover, she suggested that she would like to continue to keep in contact with Caitlin. However, Caitlin decided not to at this time. According to what her Korean mother said, Caitlin had had many siblings. As the economic situation of her family worsened, the mother had to make a decision to place Caitlin up for adoption. I was at a loss of what to say. I just could not find words to comfort her who persisted in not seeing her biological parents again. Caitlin had a happy life now. Nobody knew about the sufferings and struggles that she had to experience. Still, we were just guessing the conflicts arising in her heart. Yet, we just did not know what to say to support and comfort her. All we could do was just to pray that Caitlin could regain peace in her heart, as early as she could. I knew very well that no one could bear burdens of suffering for anyone else. I was so sure that God would make Caitlin much stronger through these tribulations, leading her to regain the direction of her life under the love of God.

February 3rd 2005, I decided to travel to Korea with Eileen's family, setting some specific plans. John used to say that he would like to visit Korea some time. Eileen, Jim, and Caitlin also were enthusiastic about visiting Korea. We, all five, planned the travel to Korea with our own respective goals. I would like to see how much Korea had changed in 21 years. John would like to visit the place his wife had been born. Caitlin also wanted to visit Korea, where she was born and her birth mother and siblings were still living. I ordered a group tour from the travel agency. Traveling from Jeju Island, through PuSan, Kyong-Ju and Sorak Mountain, we would end our travel in Seoul, where we would spend another three days. I was so inspired by my imagination of how much Korea had changed as well as my expectations of meeting my friends that I had missed so much.

February 10th 2005, it was such a spiritually nourishing moment to have a bible study with Mrs. Woo and to pray together. Although I was unable to memorize the entire verses assigned to each class, I tried to do my best to apply this Word of God to my life. On my way home after the bible study, I always ruminated on my life and the meaning of the word. I really felt encouraged and nourished by Mrs. Woo.

March 2nd 2005, there was a frigid wind as if the winter had returned. I always tried to encourage Barbara living next to me to go to church. Resolutely, she would never go to church as she was angry with God who took her husband away at a young age. I pitied her soul that bore such a distorted heart filled with hate and resentment without experiencing the love of God. The anger of this older woman was so serious that I could not address this issue to her any longer. "God! Please have mercy on her! Thaw her heart with your love!"

March 20th 2005, I got to talk to my friends living in Korea over the phone more frequently than ever. Although we had not had contact frequently, we did talk to each other once or twice a year. The ties of friendship maintained since childhood was cherished so dearly. Whenever I thought of my home country, I would always remember my friends first of all who I grew up with. They kept asking me what I would like to do when I visited Korea. So, they could make a tour plan in advance. I wanted to see Insubong Mountain again.

I used to hike up the steep path of the mountain next to Insubong, the peak of Do Bong Mountain with my friends a lot. I would like to see Insubong again if I could. It seems that it would be impossible for me to hike up that high mountain since I hadn't climbed in twenty-four years. When I was in Korea, I used to hike up the steep mountain every weekend. Whenever I climbed and stood on the peak across from Insubong, I gazed across to the next mountain which had a sheer rock face, it seemed that the rock climbers hanging ropes looked so small that their moves looked insignificant, as the rock was so gigantic in comparison with people. We used to watch those rock climbers with amazement, standing on the peak right across from the rock of Insubong they were climbing.

I also wanted to take a trip to the west coast beach of Korea. The coast of the west sea, when the tide was slowly ebbing, various rock islands would appear. It was a very beautiful beach! When I was walking with my friends, leading them as well as following them, I could see that the twilight would gradually dye our skirts and faces with the red rays of the dying sun light. The dim recollection made me miss the coast of the west sea and its scenic twilight. When the setting sun would cover the coast at its low tide, it seemed that melancholic songs of white shells resonated. The memory of sitting on the beach listening ecstatically to the sound of the sea and gazing at the horizon saturated me with a sense of nostalgia. However, my main concern was to meet my friends rather than to going sightseeing. I was also concerned about sightseeing for those who were traveling with me.

April 13th 2005, I visited a woman who was agonizing at the loss of her husband due to a serious of disease. She just seemed to be absent-minded, as she showed her reluctance to have a conversation with me. I fully understand how she might be feeling while I watched her looking down at the floor.

I could understand her confusion as well as frustration. I was compelled to share this burden of suffering with her. In order to do this, I had to expose my wounds again that I had tried to conceal. Against my will I narrated my story of suffering with composure and self-control, and then I just burst out crying, as these stories still hurt me. She held my hand, crying suddenly.

We just embraced together, sharing pains and wounds that could be felt silently. I exposed my wounds like a proud soldier would do for glory. I also tried to witness the glory of God that could be revealed in the process of God's healing of my wounds. Still, as I knew that she had to get through such an endless night of despair from now on, I was a bit sorry about the process that she had to take. I understood with endurance and perseverance the amount of suffering that God allowed was the access point to the blessing of the pathway to approach God. I prayed that she would seek the Lord more and more and that her suffering would ease with time. I also prayed that God would give her power so she can sustain her life during her sufferings.

> "Praise be to the God and Father of our Lord
> Jesus Christ, the Father of compassion and the
> God of all comfort, who comforts us in all our
> troubles, so that we can comfort those in any
> trouble with the comfort we ourselves have
> received from God (2 Corinthians 1:3-4)."

> "Blessed are the poor in spirit, for theirs is
> the kingdom of heaven (Matthew 5:3)."

May 17th 2005, we sold our house that we had lived in since J.J. had been 5 years old until he went to college. There was a scale on the wall that John had recorded the transition of the height of J.J. every 6 month from 5 years old until he was 16. He used to have J.J. stand against the wall and he would mark his height with pencil. It seemed that it was like a tape measure attached to the wall. As I gazed at the scale that would never be increased, I could not restrain my pain. From time to time, I intentionally tried to avoid looking at it. I was planning to move before J.J.s death but after he died, I had mixed feelings. Moving out of the house felt as if we were abandoning J.J. But after J.J.s death I could not confront those memories any longer so I had to move.

The house made me feel so sad whenever I looked around it. We disposed of many unnecessary things that we had stored up and gave them away, to many people. As I was packing up my household items, I came to recognize that I was greedier than I thought. I saw that there was even some stuff not unpacked in a box that I had brought in the basement 16 years before. I thought about the poor people living in many impoverished countries that I saw on T.V. There were so many destitute people in the world and I tried to possess more and more. I felt so guilty. I was so ashamed of myself because I possessed better things increasingly unsatisfied with what I had. While packing display stands, I saw that there were so many souvenirs that I had purchased from various places we had visited. Inspired by exotic tastes of the place that I traveled, I used to buy lots of souvenirs in the hope that I could seize that moment perpetually by means of buying those souvenirs. However, I could see that such attempts were so futile. Now I gazed at those souvenirs filling the display stands with a vacant and futile feeling fading away with those irretrievable recollections.

All those ornaments that brought me joy and pleasure became meaningless. While giving away those things to those who were starting a new household and neighbors who needed them, I felt truly comfortable. I felt liberated from the narrow corner of the world that I had clung to. I tried to practice abandoning various worldly things gradually. Perceiving the truth of non-possession, I tried to do my best sharing what I had with those who are in need. I recognized that there were still so many things to discard before I would go to heaven.

May 19th, 2005 I finally stepped on Korean soil that I had missed for 21 years. The new In Chon Airport welcomed me in its new and wonderful ways. Five of my friends came to the airport to see me. As one of them did not have a chance to visit me in the U.S with the rest of my other friends, I saw her for the first time in nearly 21 years. At first, I could not recognize her. I felt so sorry about it and tried to do my best to excuse myself. As I entered the city of Seoul, I could see many high-rise apartments throughout the city. Now I could see the so-called forest of high-rise apartments. The Han River seemed to flow beautifully as it had done before but now in a more arranged and organized way since my youth.

Once again, I felt how fast time flies. Each of us had changed as time went by. Our appearance had changed as we felt the weight of years. We hadn't seen each other for many years but we chatted just as if I had seen them yesterday. We were the same as the young girls chatting endlessly. We arrived at our lodgings located in the Guest House of Tower Palace. The Thompson family, Jim, Eileen and Caitlin, lodged in a room equipped in a Korean style without any bed. I suggested changing the room with us as they might feel uncomfortable with the Korean style.

But they insisted on sleeping in a Korean style. As I laid out the Korean quilts, they were enthusiastic about its beauty and comfort. These rooms were very comfortable and cozy. Even the thought that I was in my mother land made me feel very comfortable, as if I were in a motherly bosom.

May 20th 2005, the Kang Nam district where we were staying was newly organized, it was clean and beautiful. I felt little bit distanced from it. On the other hand, the old-fashioned market of Nam Dae Moon and Myung Dong district were so familiar and comfortable to me as if I had come to my home town, in spite of their antiquated appearance. I even found the old-fashioned café and restaurant that was still there where I used to go to with my friends. It was reminiscent of the past days of my youth. I was deeply immersed in those recollections. My friends guided our group alternately, revealing our tight ties of friendship. I was so proud and thankful for my friends.

I found myself calculating the equivalent of a dollar to the Korean won for payment. I just realized that I had become a person who priced things only through an American dollar. Moreover, I just kept using English unconsciously. I found myself neither fully a Korean, nor fully an American. I could sense that I had already been Americanized, as I came to realize some cultural differences between me and other Koreans, which I could not realize in the U.S. I finally came to be an ambiguous stranger who is neither a Korean in Korea, nor an American in America. I suddenly felt loneliness. I deeply understand that I was just a perpetual wanderer no matter where I traveled. Suddenly, there was a voice resonating in my heart. "You are the one who possesses the eternal life!" Neither Korea, nor America, is my home. They are just a place that I came to visit under the plan of God who created me. My final destination is nothing but the heaven. I was born anew into life ever blessed and never exchangeable for another. I lived every day with such a heart trembling with grace, overwhelmed with such a passionate thankfulness.

May 31ˢᵗ, 2005 after staying for two days in Seoul, we took a tour around Korea, through Jeju Island, Pusan, Kyung Joo, Sorak Mountain, and finally back to Seoul again. I wanted to stay a few more days and had lots of regrets that I could not do more, I was so sorry about leaving for the U.S so early.

Caitlin began to cry, as some emotion surged up within her. Would it be a sense of guilt that she refused to see her birth mother and siblings while she had stayed in Korea? Or, was it a sense of sorrow that she had to be adopted against her will, detached from her family and Korea? Who could guess those delicate residues of her sufferings and sorrows that may reside in her deepest thoughts? I hugged her and prayed in such a way. "Dear God! Please heal her wounds and bless her life with your care." I also felt some sorrow about parting from my friends again, in my deepest part of my heart. I had experienced many different forms of encounters and separations. Every separation was very hard for me. That night, I could not sleep well, full of a mixture of emotions.

Chapter Fourteen

Hope-Inspiration of Life

"Teach us to number our days aright, that we
may gain a heart of wisdom (Psalm 90:12)."

June 5th 2005, I felt little bit exhausted for three days after I had come back from Korea. John seemed to cope with the jet lag. However, I was more affected by it. I would fall asleep at 7 o'clock in the evening. When I woke up, it took time to realize that I was home. Those recent memories in Korea seemed to fade away as if it had happened long time ago. I realized that my life would fade away like a dream in such a short time so I determined to devote my life for the mission of serving the eternal kingdom of God. Above all, I had to humble myself every moment. I could not but deny that pride was always rearing its ugly head, which made me feel more dejected. Nevertheless, my firm assurance that God would not abandon me but mold me in his forgiveness and love even in the time of my despair and disappointment inspired my life with hope.

July 30th, 2005 when I woke up, I remembered that it was J.J.'s birthday. As I got out of bed and opened the curtain, I could see the crystal-clear sky unblemished without any cloud in sight. I wrote a letter to J.J. "Dear J.J. I came to have the second birthday of yours without your presence. You were my pleasure, as your presence always made my life toward you joyful as well as rewarding. I am just trying to stand erect in the world without your presence, gazing upon the sky with my firm standing. Even today, when the intense rays of the sun hit me, the bread of life from heaven comes down on me. Hope! It is like an inspiration that puts life into my spirit. My hope is that this life is not an end but that I could meet you in another life is really inspiring the inexpressible joy and gratefulness gushing out of my graced heart. He was the one who came to the world in the form of a human for the sake of those sinful creatures and bore the cross on his back! How can we even imagine such an infinite love beyond human capacity? I really would like to live like a flower created by him that may yield a beautiful fragrance in a corner of the earth even though it may be reserved and shy.

Every evening, I may be frustrated at my incorrigible habits persisting in my life. Nevertheless, I never give up the hope that I may be sanctified according to his image. It is because my Lord will not give up on me......J.J. when I think of your name, my heart gets an unbearable longing for you. On the other hand, I am still surrounded with joy whenever I think of the heaven where you are residing. As I gaze to the sky, it seemed that I could see you running around with joy. That made me smile. This joy that God planted in my heart removes all tears and pain from me and surely belongs in heaven. I love you forever, Mom!" The Lord embraced my heart passionately today. My love for God grows and I want to praise the lord with all my being.

"Love the Lord your God with all your heart
and with all your soul and with all your mind
and with all your strength (Mark 12:30)."

August 1ˢᵗ 2005, I met a young man today and when I was talking to him, I found out he doesn't have any dreams for the future. That made me realize; that I don't really have concrete dreams any more. I felt that God was refining me through sufferings of love. Moreover, I also felt myself maturing. I could sympathize with the pains of others. I believe that this gift of sympathy enabling me to be with those who are suffering was flowing out of the grace and bliss that God was instilling into my heart. I thought that those moments of tribulations were changed to be an instrument through which I could hold the hands of those who were suffering. I could see that they were also opening their hearts to me, by means of this instrument. "Can I only live for God, glorifying him only?" I was deeply engrossed with only one concern which is how I can please God like a lover who tried to please his/her beloved. I tried to do my best to listen to the voice of the Lord. Although I could not hear a voice that could be heard through the ears, I still could sense what the will of God directed to me, would be from deep within my soul. God did not want me to create a huge change in the world, but wanted me to live faithfully by acting on the slightest thing assigned to me and to be obedient to the word of God.

"But to each one of us grace has been given as Christ apportioned it (Ephesians 4:7)" God made me to be aware of this simple truth.

"Please help me to approach with the heart of Christ those who are suffering!" I prayed that this simple purpose might motivate my whole life and I would be one of those who would bring the hope and the comfort of heaven to others ignorant of this truth. September 3rd 2005, the calling that you assigned.

As embraced in precious life.
Sincere affection with all people.
Bears good fruit in beautiful valleys.
My heart sees the beautiful garden.
Toward the beautiful sky beyond the hill crest.
Telling them with passion that their sufferings hey experienced.
Are really the love of Christ who are risking his flesh.
I could see the beautiful garden where you are staying.
Toward the beautiful sky beyond abrupt hills.
I am stepping nearer and nearer.
The flakes of grace coming from the sky.
The flakes of grace falling like magnificent rays of the sun.
Along the sky of crystal, clear and transparent, spreading over the wings of the soul about to float with joy.
I fly toward the highest.
In the form of the shapeless wind.
Lord, I am really thankful to you for letting me meet such a precious brother.

September 12th 2005, would I have looked toward the Lord, if I had not experienced such suffering? I just wondered whether I would have detached from those earthly passions and instinct without such suffering. I was still worrying about a lot of things. But my worrying was far less than previously.

As I made my heart devoid of earthly yearning, I felt my heart filled with other joys. I could see that there were many people lonely and in pain around me, those I had not been able to see before. And I could sense that God was matching me with many people who had pain. As I met many people, they felt that they were not alone in their suffering and got some comfort from my stories, I was grateful to God for making me an instrument of comfort.

October 19, 2005 our new house is a town house. Driving down the road toward the house we could see poplar trees arranged on the both sides of the road as columns. The houses were built behind the trees. In the middle of the road leading from the entrance, there was a slope on a hill paved with asphalt. While driving on that road, I felt that this slope on the hill seemed to be a road to the sky. This slope paved with asphalt seems like the horizon where the sky and the earth meet, at least as seen from the inside of the car through the windshield. Whenever I was driving home, the road always presented such a beautiful and inspiring scene each evening, where the sky embroidered with clouds would show variegated colors reflecting the twilight.

On a sunny day, the sky without any single trace of clouds always suggested the blue ocean in my imagination. It seemed that I would fall into the water of the ocean if I would pass over the top of the hill. On other days, the sky tinged with silvery clouds always reminded me of fine soft fluffy feathers floating in the sky. So, I imagined myself banished beyond the clouds, disappearing in them. In the twilight, the evening glow that tinges the sky with the red flames of the sun always dazzled me, with its magnificence as well as melancholy. On the way home calling it a day, I found myself gazing into the sky; I can still confess life is sometimes tearful and painful but this world is still beautiful.

November 8th 2005, I met Mrs. Kim whom I had come to know by chance on account of my business. She looked less healthy than she had in the previous few months. She appeared with short hair, adding that her hair was falling out nowadays because of her medical treatment. I stood aghast, staring at her. She said that she had been fine for two years since the surgery for gastric cancer. However, she said that it recurred recently and she had to have some radiation treatments.

She said that her doctor reported that she could live only six months at best. She told me these things so calmly. I could not find the words to respond. I sat still with my head down. She worried about her son above all, who was not married yet. Seeing the heart of a mother who worried about the future of her son in spite of her impending death, I felt my heart torn apart by sorrow. "Oh! It was such a heartbreaking and difficult separation!" I just sighed in my heart we could not continue our conversation any more as we were choked with sorrows.

On the way home, I kept pondering about what I would do if I had only 6 months to live. Ascertaining that I had to be more faithful to the time given to each day, I reflected on whether I did my best devoting my time to God faithfully. I went to my loft and knelt in prayer. "Teach us to number our days aright, that we may gain a heart of wisdom (Psalm 90:12)." November 23, 2005.

Thanksgiving Day! There is an American church within a forty-minute drive from my house. This church would provide a thanksgiving dinner to those who did not have anywhere to go. We decided to join that program and server dinner instead of being with our family members. At around 3PM, about

50 people came and took their places at the table. Those who were handicapped, those who had mental disorders, and those who were homeless......We were shocked at the fact that there were so many people around us who did not have any place to go. Serving and then sitting and eating among them, the soul of each person seemed to be so precious and appealing to me. I prayed that the spirit of Christ would be incorporated into their beings just as those meals were and would nourish their spirits with spiritual food. We went there to share our love. However, we came back with our love increased and flourished. On the way home, I looked up to a night sky with twinkling stars spread in it. There, I came to recognize that the love of Christ was also shining like a jewel in my heart like those stars glimmering in the sky.

December 10th, 2005 Pastor Lee, who was in charge of the Philadelphia branch of Mil-Al Mission Association, organized a program titled "A Class of Love" every Saturday, in order to provide some weekly rest to the parents of those children with disabilities. He was taking care of these children, and worshipping with them. Although he was disabled, he was serving these children with a big smile full of love. I felt greatly influenced by his services. Today, we prepared a lunch for them and visited with the disabled class. It seemed that the class was full of happiness, as most of the children were very innocent.

The pastor explained that they looked happy because they did not get stressed. I could see that the pastor, his wife, and volunteer staff members were living a Christian life. A happy atmosphere was overflowing from that class.

January 2nd, 2006, I went to the Maryland Retreat Center located near Chesapeake Bay, in order to participate in the fasting revival meeting hosted for the first two days of every

New Year season by my church. This retreat center was managed very well, equipped with 150 rooms and various facilities for different programs. Other than some Korean immigrant churches, many American churches used this center. I wanted to be "renewed in body, soul, and mind" as a brochure stated.

I could see a large sign, on which the phrase "Jesus never fails!" was inscribed. I replied to this phrase by saying "Amen!" While preaching the sermon "How to Pray" Pastor Lee talked about prayer. He taught us to pray to make ourselves live a life proper to that of a saint called by God, to pray to give a spiritual discernment in reliance in the Holy Spirit concerning God's will, and finally to pray to give us more power to do God's work as well as to endure difficulties with joy.

Waking up in the morning and taking a walk along the beach, very thick fog covered the bay. Although the bay was covered by fog, I was so certain of the existence of the bay behind the fog. Likewise, I seemed to be certain of the existence of heaven, although the heaven looked blurred with fog. I tried to listen to what God would tell me in this serene beach that seemed to be insulated from the world. I also prayed that God would mold my life to be a good vessel for him. The refreshing fog that had not cleared easily soaked my heart with grace, just as it covered the sky.

January 26th, 2006 John and I visited a mountain villa, departing from our daily routines. There was a resort area of the Pocono Mountains. It was such a famous resort area that there were many hotels located around this place. We planned to lodge in a small hotel that looked like a villa. There was a gas fireplace glowing like kindled charcoals that brought some coziness to the wintry night. We just wrote down our confessions to God with sincerity. Then, we also wrote down some directions of life that we would take. We then swapped our writings with each other.

It seemed that many aspects of our life which were purely directed toward secular values before the death of J.J. were greatly changed. We could see that we both tried to approach toward the spiritual kingdom of God as we read from the writings written by each. What was amazing was that our goals in life came to be synchronized. J.J.'s death opened our eyes and hearts to other people, the virtues that are be shared between us, delivered us out of such a myopia that just considered just our own lives. Moreover, his death also brought us to realize the reason why we were living.

I still could sense John agonizing over his wounds that were not yet fully healed. I prayed that his wounds could be healed completely and some beautiful trace of life would be revealed out of those wounds totally cured.

Chapter Fifteen

From the One who was Comforted to the One who Comforts

"Who comforts us in all our troubles, so that we can comfort those in any trouble with the comfort we ourselves have received from God (2 Corinthians 1:4)." February 17th 2006.

I received a call from Lee in the early morning. She said that she called me as she felt so frustrated. She asked me to meet her in the afternoon. Remembering her remarks that she had considered a divorce from her husband, I met her with some worries.

After eating lunch, I brought her to the Amish Village located in the Lancaster County. The Amish people were the immigrants who had migrated from Holland, Germany, and Switzerland, seeking the freedom of faith. They were living by farming in their own village, and they have their own schools and churches preserving their own cultural and religious traditions. They refused to use any modern convenience. They only used buggies drawn by horses. The idyllic scene of the Amish village was really beautiful and it always gave me peace. I kept listening to what Lee was telling me.

As the life of immigrants in the U.S demanded a really busy life, immigrants usually did not have many chances of talking with each other. Therefore, most of people tended to keep talking without listening. This time, I opted to just listen to her as much as possible, until she released her tension. She was complaining about her irresponsible husband. She was also doing her best to keep the family together. I felt her tears so precious and beautiful.

On the way home, she said that she would do her best once again, adding that her suffering was just nothing in comparison with mine. I thought that God would change the heart of the husband of Lee who was trying to endure and persevere.

March 2nd, 2006 God allowed me to meet the pastor Ho Yon Lee. It seemed that the pastor shed the fragrance of Christ even from his gentle smile and humble attitude. When he was teaching the panorama of the Scripture and preaching the Word of God, we could sense how excited he was by the passion and love of God. It was really a stimulating experience. The pastor urged us to reflect on how much time we were devoting to the Lord and whether we were living faithful to the mission assigned to us. His message really provided a chance for me to reexamine my life.

After having lost J.J., I had been committed to praying for and promoting those youths living with difficulties as well as the children of missionaries. I was so glad that I could meet a pastor who shared the same concerns as me. I felt that I and the pastor seemed to share the same spiritual concern. I told the pastor while we were having lunch together that I had been writing my confession. The pastor told me that suffering allowed by God would be within God's plan for those who were sympathizing with those who might also suffer in a similar situation.

By his teaching, I could hold fast my wishes of prayers devoted to God more firmly than ever.

March 17th, 2006

Out of the spring of joy embedded in my heart.
The love is springing ceaselessly.
I thank you Lord for shaping me to share this love.
I also thank you Lord for shaping me perceive
Even those tiny wild flowers are your grace.
I also thank you Lord for shaping me kindled with the passion.
The passion of the sun in the twilight burning all the universe.
with its light.
I also thank you Lord for bringing rain onto the field parched
with thirst.
For wiping tears with your grace.
I also thank you Lord for saturating my soul with dews of grace.
For being surrounded in your blessings.
Toward the heaven that I see with my eyes closed.
Until the end of my life when my respiration expires.
With my soul saturated with your dazzling scents.
I am dreaming my soul to be dedicated to you Lord.

Not being afraid of separating myself from the world Is because
of the faith that I am heading toward my destination.

April 6th, 2006 John decided to volunteer for a program called Habitat for Humanity of Montgomery County, which helped to repair and fix some worn-down houses or build new homes for low-income residents. It was a volunteer service that J.J. had done once or twice while he had been home during the summer vacation. Moreover, it was also the thing that John had wanted to do for some time. He said that he made up his mind and would start this in May. God finally cured his wounds and made him yield a precious fruit of serving his neighbor. I prayed with thankfulness that he may yield more and more fruits.

December 1st, 2006 there was an announcement that John's company would have a massive laying-off. The company encouraged some volunteers to retire voluntarily before the announcement of the laying off program. It was said that there would be some benefits for voluntary resignations. John assumed that he might be laid off as he worked for the company for a long time. However, John was also afraid that he might not be able to pay off the mortgages that were unfinished. We pondered this issue for a while. We concluded that a large amount of money was not necessary for the basic sustenance of life. It seemed that we tried to acquire more money by working because we did not want to leave the comfortable life, because of our greed. I had felt somewhat guilty that we were too preoccupied with the matter of sustenance, investing time and energy, without offering to work for the Lord. I suggested that John make a decision for the life following the Word of God through faith.

"But seek first his kingdom and his righteousness, and all

these things will be given to you as well (Matthew 6:33)." We tried to hold fast this word and prayed. We could sense that God was shaping our hearts to focus more on prayers and services in our given life.

It was a real advance for John in terms of his spiritually, to leave everything to God entirely and to make the decision to quit his job, when there was no visible plan for the future. It was such a remarkable decision and a significant change for John. On the one hand, we were little bit apprehensive of our future. We realized that our life would be experienced by living the life led by the Holy Spirit; as well as driven by his power; we felt a really jubilant expectation of the future that God had planned to provide for us.

> "Now the Jordan is at flood stage all during
> harvest. Yet as soon as the priests who carried
> the ark reached the Jordan and their feet
> touched the water's edge, the water from
> upstream stopped flowing. (Joshua 3:15:16)"

I stopped reading emotionally filled with the spirit and decided to read aloud this verse. I just tried to hold my breath, not able to finish reading and totally felt overwhelmed by this grace. In contrast with the priests who placed their feet in the water, I found myself hesitating to put my feet onto the water. Without any single hesitation, I made a determination. "Oh! God who is leading my life! Please make me to be obedient to your plan with faith!" At that place, I resolutely put my feet into the water of faith flowing like a river of life, leaving my life to God's hand. Finally, I felt myself deeply immersed in that water of grace.

January 15th, 2007 I was reading a book titled "There is always enough". It was a story about a missionary couple who had volunteered to go to Mozambique which lacked any trace of civilized life. They practiced the love of Jesus for any children abandoned and starving in horrible conditions. I was totally affected by their witnesses. I was so moved and entirely immersed in their story all day long. I could see that God was still doing his best in not missing any single soul that may seem to be abandoned at the edge of the earth as well as embracing each with his infinite love. I came to understand fully that some super human power was overflowing from their missionary life with spiritual dynamism infused by the assistance of the Holy Spirit.

April 18th 2007, I came to hear about the Ezmiah Movement from Pastor Sun Kun Lee. Ezmiah Movement is abbreviated from the Ezra-Nehemiah Movement that intends to promote contributions to Korean society and church, Ezra fostered the spiritual reconstitution of his mother land as well as Nehemiah supported the political and social reconstitution of his mother land. It was said that there were around 6.7 to 7 million Korean immigrants scattered among 5000 churches and in 180 countries. They seemed to be like Diaspora Jews in a modern Korean version.

Specifically, this program tried to promote various second-generation Koreans to revitalize Korean society by making them visit Korea and involve themselves in the development of agricultural communities, like Nehemiah. This program also intended to promote them to regenerate the spiritual condition of the rural church like Ezra, by asking them to serve at summer and winter bible schools offered in English at rural churches. Moreover, this program also strives to help them rediscover their cultural and ethnic roots and to be spiritual leaders to their peers when they return to the U.S. I decided to participate as a member of the Ezmiah team and I prepared for it.

May 30th, 2007 God provided a small business for me. I was thankful to God that I was able to have a business that I could enjoy in collaboration with Mr. Min Ho Park and his wife, with whom I had a close fellowship in Christ. Passing through the Old Eagle School Road surrounded by dense and shady trees, to get to my store located on Conestoga Road; which was also dense with trees. While driving, I usually kept the car windows open so that I could drink the smell of the forest. The refreshing odor of morning foliage flowing from trees reaching to the sky as well as from shrubs soaked with dew always helped me get rid of those bitter roots left in my soul. I was able to start every day with happiness. I drove to the store praising God with an open heart, thinking that God planned and organized everything so considerately that he could allow me to start a daily routine with such joy.

June 1st 2007, I met Eileen and explained about the Ezmiah Movement and my plan to visit Korea again. Eileen, confessed that her life had been full of joy because of her adopted daughter Caitlin from Korea. She said that she always wanted to pay back Korea for the gift that she received (her daughter). She said that she would like to come with me. On that day Eileen and I decided to visit Korea again.

June 23rd 200, I received a notice from the pastor Ho Yon Lee that we would be dispatched to a certain orphanage in Yang Pyong city with another team. Eileen and I purchased some gifts for the children in the orphanage as well as some teaching materials for the English Camp program offered at the orphanage. Moreover, I prayed to God every evening that

I would be filled with a clean and passionate heart filled with the love of Christ before I would meet the children.

July 17th, 2007 as I got off the airplane at Inchon Airport, it was really humid because it was the rainy season. I could see the wife of the pastor waiting for me, who had gentle eyes like a deer. I was so glad to see her that I embraced her. Following her direction to go to a particular spot in the airport, I could see other members of the group waiting for us. It seemed that we might be those who arrived last. Various people from other places in the U.S. were gathering. Most of them seemed to be young high school or college kids and some of them seemed to be their pastors, parents, and staff members.

Then, we moved to the Team Retreat Center located in Bulgwang District of Seoul by bus. As it got darker, we could not recognize where we were. But as I could see some neon signboards lighting and flickering, I felt familiar with these scenes because they were the same that I had been accustomed to in Korea before coming to the U.S. Arriving at the retreat center, we were met by Pastor Bo Gil Kang and his wife as well as my friend Nam Joo who greeted us. After Eileen and I put our possessions in our lodgings, they took us to a restaurant where we had a good dinner and cordial conversation. That night in my home country, where I have many friends to welcome me, felt like the bosom of a mother and I fell asleep, hearing a murmuring brook.

July 19th, 2007 waking up early and looking out the window, I could see Buk-Han Mountain appearing like a picture. I was now seeing a very high mountain right in front of my lodging in the midst of the big city. It was such an unbelievable scene, a clear and fresh brook flowing from the mountain sounded like a sweet rainy rush to my ears. Before we were dispatched to the mission field, we were supposed to have a revival meeting that would last for three days. I could see many students coming from very remote countries as well as from the U.S and Canada. In spite of exhaustion caused by jet-lag, the early morning worship service elicited a real enthusiasm among participants about joining in the work of the Lord in unity with the Holy Spirit. The slogan of the program was "Beyond Borders! Beyond Races!".

Participants were grouped by divisions. We were in charge of the program that taught English Bible School. Our team was dispatched to the orphanage, "Shin Mang Won," and consisted of Susan, Chardaie, Tom, Kim, Eileen and myself. I was in charge of drawing pictures and making crafts. I kept practicing and reviewing my lessons. On day two, we had two other members, Dr. Park and her daughter, join us. She said that she had been doing volunteer work in Africa. During the day, I once grumbled that it was so hot in this lodging. Dr. Park replied that this lodging would have been one of the best hotels in Africa where she was a missionary, saying that sometimes she had to sleep in the jungle. Listening to what she said, I thought that her faithful service devoted to so many people was really beautiful. I also felt ashamed of my grumbling and impatience about the inconveniences.

July 20th, 2007 while preaching a service, Pastor Lee said that many newly divorced couples sent their children to their grandparents who lived in rural areas. He said that these children were suffering from a double shock, the separation from their parents as well the isolation from their familiar urban lives. Who can cure the sufferings of so many children?

"Oh Lord!" A deep sigh came out of my heart, as I thought of those children in pain because of the selfishness of their parents. We felt so sore in our hearts; Eileen and I wept so much. We the teams of the "Ezmiah Program" were supposed to travel to remote rural places as well as isolated islands to serve these disenfranchised children with the help of Summer English Bible School programs. I prayed that the lord's healing hands can reach out to them.

July 21ˢᵗ, 2007 Eileen and I met Caitlin's birthmother in the evening. Pastor Lee, arranged the meeting. We were led to a certain Korean restaurant. At first the two mothers of Caitlin were at a loss of what to say. They just kept reiterating "Thank you so much" again and again. I told Caitlin's birthmother, that Caitlin would be successful in society because she had been raised with such caring love. I tried to comfort her because of her possible feelings of shame. I also tried to interpret every single word that they were communicating, trying to tell them what they were implying, i.e., what they could not express explicitly. Who could even guess the complicated emotions and feelings that might be going through their minds? While interpreting what they said to each other, I wished that Eileen's intention to relieve the guilty feeling of Caitlin's birthmother could be clearly communicated to her. Eileen said that she could be free from her pain inside her heart as much as she could.

I thought about what she went through sending her baby to a remote country to enable her daughter to experience a better life. It was such a difficult situation and must have been really hard. Eileen held her hand. Her birthmother said thank you to Eileen for raising her daughter with great love. The two mothers held hands tightly and warmly, instead of specifying their feelings stored up for such a long time.

Chapter Sixteen

Spreading Over the Wings of Grace

July 23rd, 2007 as soon as I had entered the orphanage "Shin Mang Won (the garden of faith and hope)" I was so inspired by the sounds of the children's playing. On the way to our lodging though the corridor, we passed a room in which six babies were staying. As soon as we had put our personal items in our lodging, Eileen and I went back to that room. We helped some of the staff with giving the babies baths and changing their clothes. One two-year old baby boy Jin Woo ran to me with his book and tried to nestle in my bosom. He called me "mom," pressing me to look at his book. By this one small word, he just captivated me. Jin Woo called me that small word which I thought I would never hear again. Feeling that I became truly his mother, I held him tight and said; "I really would like to be your mom, and to remember and pray for you in the rest of my life. If God allows, I hope I could come to this place every year and see how you may grow…"

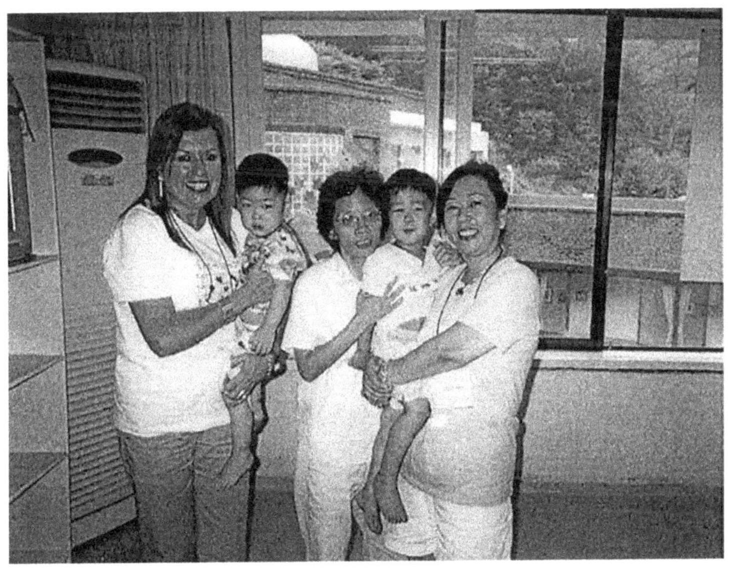

Jin Woo talked really well, Jin Young was a really talented imp, Jae-Il was a really big baby, Eun Song cried all the time and wanted to be embraced. Eun Song kept crying and asking for attention from the caregiver, who was taking care of all six babies graciously. We were totally overwhelmed by her loving as well as efficient care.

The orphanage had approximately fifty children aged three months old until they were 18 years old. The kids were all cheerful. They would sometimes fight with each other. However, they got along together really well forgetting about their previous hassles and played together just like brother and sisters. They reminded me of my own childhood. It was so good to see that the older children like elder brothers and sisters would help the younger children work out their arguments.

July 24th 2007 in the early morning around 6 o'clock, tunes of God's praises were heard flowing out of loud speakers and woke us up from our sweet dreams. I could see that many children were waking up, yawning and coming out of their respective rooms along the long the corridor. There was a room with long wash stands installed and many taps arranged in a line with a wide trough covered with ceramic tiles. As I looked through a large window right above the wash stands, I could see a very verdant forest spreading out in front of the building. I also could hear a brook murmuring through the forest. I was so fascinated at such a beautiful scene, while washing up for the day.

At 6:30, we gathered and offered a service lead by Mister Kim. Each of the group read a verse alternately. I thought that God would remember these souls trying to devote their morning time to Him, and bless them for their entire life.

We sang a song together "Dear gracious God offering us meals every day!" in front of meal tables. Those young children gathered, folding their tiny hands and singing loudly together. On those breakfast tables, God's smile seemed to shine down on them with dazzling sunshine. Singing aloud the song that I had long ago forgotten; I was really grateful to God for allowing me a chance to be with these children.

We taught the children some scriptural verses and praises in English as well as help them draw pictures and make some crafts until 9 P.M. Chardaie, who was from Africa and a Harvard senior, came to Korea to do volunteer work during the summer. While teaching English, she tried to inspire courage and hope in the children, saying that they also could go to Harvard if they would study and pray hard. Normally Chardaie taught advanced English, while the rest of the group taught very basic English words through some games. Moreover, we encouraged them to memorize very simple Bible verses every class. Even very young children ignorant of our alphabet memorized and recited with the older children some verses such as "for the Lord your God is with you wherever you go".

All the children in our group memorized and sang the English praises that I liked the most on the last day of camp. Their zeal to absorb everything they had learned was so outstanding. They were like thirsty trees in the summer absorbing rain quickly. Likewise, they were also trying to stand firm like those healthy green trees outside the building.

> You are my Strength when I am weak
>
> You are the treasure that I seek
>
> You are my all in all Seeking
>
> You as a precious jewel.
>
> Lord, to give up I'd be a fool
>
> You are my all in all
>
> Jesus, Lamb of God,
>
> Worthy is your name.
>
> Taking my sin, my cross, my shame.
>
> Raising up again, I bless your name.
>
> You are my all in all.
>
> When I fall down You pick me up. When I am dry, you fill my cup.
>
> You are my all in all
>
> With my arms up joyfully, I praised God with these children.

July 26th, 2007 thinking that I did not have many days until we would have to leave, I felt really uneasy about the separation. It seemed that these children of Shin Mang Won did not care about the separation, because they were used to it. I did not know how many groups which had visited the orphanage and promised to come again would keep their promises. I thought that these children tried to protect themselves from getting hurt by pretending to be nonchalant about visitors leaving them. I hoped that I would come to this place again. But I did not make any promises. I just tried to inscribe all these children into my heart and take all of them into my memory. We made many teddy bears and encouraged the children to write down their wishes in English as well as in Korean on small paper notes and then put them into the pockets of the teddy bears. We told them to embrace those bears while praying for their wishes when they slept at night. I wrote down their wishes on behalf of the young ones. A child told me that her wish was for her mother to come back and see her again. This broke my heart. Other children wrote down their wishes such as being a football player or a teacher and so forth. I could not help but smile as I thought that God had planned fabulous futures for these children.

August 16th, 2007 Pastor Ho Yon Lee explained that he was planning a Youth Vision School that would promote the self-esteem in forty youths who were making a livelihood on their own. He believed that this identity building might lead them to live valuable lives. If we would live according to the direction that God wanted us to live, then God's will, would be realized through the dream of his people. As soon as I had listened to his plan, I came to understand that God was realizing the wishes of my prayer through Pastor Lee. I also thought that many youths who did not have parents suffered such financial difficulties and could be reborn into true children of God who would help others. They would endure these difficulties with the dream of the kingdom of God. I totally agreed with the pastor's plan and ministry and decided to participate in it.

God blessed me with the hope to meet more spiritual

children in the future. I was really grateful and praised God, as I knew that in all things God works for the good and according to his purpose. The providence of God was creating harmony and established goodness in all.

August 17th 2007, I participated in a revival meeting led by Pastor Yoo. I had wanted to participate in a spiritual exercise program called "Tres Dias" which was a Christian renewal movement. There I experienced the presence of the Holy Spirit in my life and worshipped with my entire being.

All the people gathered thcir worshipped God, united into one heart as all were inspired by the Holy Spirit. I worshipped God with the praises that were flowing out of my heart. My heart was filled with the Holy Spirit and I sang:

I raise my hands up to You, Lord.

You are worthy of praises. I opened my hearts to you

You are worthy of praises.

Delight instead of sadness

Crown of beauty instead of ashes.

Praise instead of anxiety

Make me clothed with praises.

September 1st 2007

I reflect on those days.

When I was unable to get out of the swamp of despair.

Standing at the edge of the cliff in a haze.

I wantcd to fly once again, resorting to his care.

The Lord gently held my hands.

He gave me wings to soar up high.

So, I could soar up to his place.

The wings of grace under the name of hope.
Following the path that he determined.
Joyfully flying spreading the wings of grace.
Someday when I depart from earth.
Taking off the weight of my burden.
I will go up toward his place.
The one who created me with his everlasting love.
The eternal place of the everlasting rest,
Where my son and other beloveds are resting...
Toward that place, I raise my hands, praising God.
My spirit will fly toward heaven.
Soaring up to the high and high to the eternal place.

"You turned my wailing into dancing; you removed my sackcloth and clothed me with joy, that my heart may sing to you and not be silent. O LORD my God, I will give you thanks forever (Psalm 30:11 -12)."

Through all the tribulations allowed under God's providence, I came to acquire a sight that can reach to heaven as well as merciful hands that could heal many wounds. At the moment when I could not even make a slight groaning sound because the suffering was so severe, God also poured out his love painfully to me which enabled me to fly spreading the wings for a more magnificent vision. I wish to imitate Christ who served many homeless and poor people in this world as well as to be shaped according to the image that God wants me to embody.

I had a chance to read The Vision Statement of these youths who participated in Youth Vision School organized by Ho Yon Lee. Our dreams that God wants to realize in our lives were embedded in each dream of these youths. We tried to be nurturing soil that can provide nourishment so that the roots of faith of these promising youths can be rooted deeply. We have to register our group as a non-profit organization in order to help those children living in Korea in a more effective way. We are in the process of registering under the title of "Hopeful Vision".

Continuously, I am offering my praise and
gratefulness to God, my potter who has shaped me
into the one who is dreaming to fly in a changed
life of newness with a humble heart. "For it is God
who works in you to will and to act according
to his good purpose. (Philippians 2:13)."

-The End-